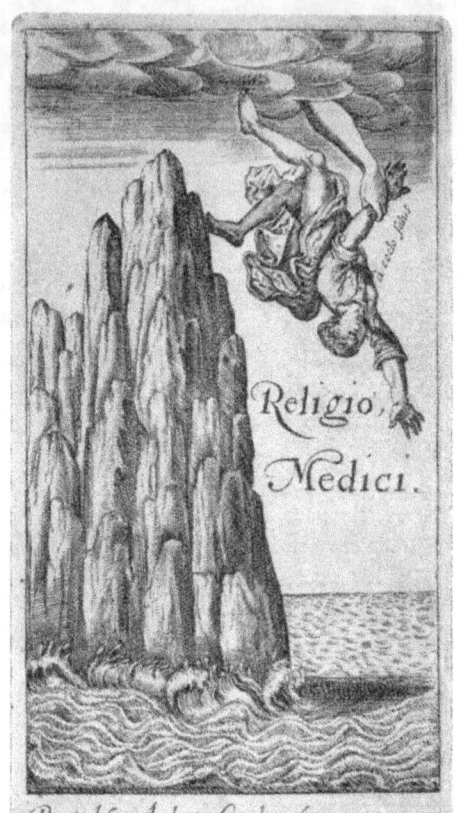

Sir Thomas Browne

*A Study in
Religious Philosophy*

by

WILLIAM P. DUNN

The University of Minnesota Press
MINNEAPOLIS

Copyright 1950 by the
UNIVERSITY OF MINNESOTA

All rights reserved. No part of this book may be reproduced in any form without the written permission of the publisher. Permission is hereby granted to reviewers to quote brief passages in a review to be printed in a magazine or newspaper.

LONDON · GEOFFREY CUMBERLEGE · OXFORD UNIVERSITY PRESS

To E. S. D.

Foreword

IN preparing this book for a second edition, I felt that an extensive revision was called for. It was necessary to correct a number of errors and to take account of some important recent contributions to the study of Sir Thomas Browne. But I wanted also, to a certain extent at least, to bring the book into line with various changes in my own opinions and tastes since 1926, when it was first printed. Accordingly I have recast some parts of it, entirely rewritten others, and made a good many minor excisions and additions throughout.

In quoting from Browne I have used the definitive text of the Geoffrey Keynes edition (1928–31), but to facilitate reference to other editions I have generally cited passages by chapter and section only. For the same reason, where there are page references to the Keynes edition, in the case of Browne's letters and minor works, I have also given the corresponding reference to the Wilkin edition, in the Bohn Library reprint.

After some hesitation I have modernized the spelling and capitalization of the Keynes text and those of all seventeenth-century authors quoted, both for prose and poetry. Many will feel that contemporary forms are part of a writer's literary personality and cannot be changed without loss. On the other hand, for the general reader obsolete spellings are a distraction and produce a certain feeling of unreality. It has seemed best in a book of this kind to defer to the latter point of view.

During the last twenty-five years interest in Sir Thomas Browne has been active and wide-ranging. Among many books and articles, some of which are referred to in these pages, I have found most valuable Olivier Leroy's *Le Chevalier Thomas Browne* (1931), Basil Willey's *Seventeenth Century Background* (1934), and Douglas Bush's *English Literature in the Earlier Seventeenth Century* (1945). The last has enlarged my understanding of the whole range of seventeenth-century English thought and literary art in more ways than I can easily acknowledge.

I am under long-standing obligations to Professors Huntington Brown, Samuel H. Monk, and Marjorie Nicolson for their active interest in the republication of this book, and to Margaret S. Harding, Director of the University of Minnesota Press, for undertaking it. Mr. Monk and Mr. Brown have read the manuscript and given me the benefit of their advice on a number of points. I wish also to express my special thanks to Doris E. Franklin, of the Minnesota Press staff, for valuable criticism, and to Richard S. Dunn for almost indispensable help, under trying circumstances, with research and the preparation of the manuscript.

Grateful acknowledgment is made to the following publishers for permission to quote from copyrighted books: Faber and Faber, Ltd., *The Works of Sir Thomas Browne*; Benziger Brothers, Inc., *The Summa Theologica of Thomas Aquinas*; the Soncino Press, Ltd., *The Zohar*; the Oxford University Press, *English Literature in the Earlier Seventeenth Century*, by Douglas Bush; and the Harvard University Press, *The Meditations of Marcus Aurelius*.

W. P. D.

Contents

Chapter I. THE WORLD OF SIR THOMAS BROWNE
    I. The New and the Old in Browne 3
    II. His Relation to His Century 10
    III. Some of His Interests and Activities 20
    IV. The Aim and Scope of This Book 34

Chapter II. FAITH AND REASON
    I. Browne's Religious Temperament 37
    II. Religious Liberalism in Seventeenth-Century
       England 45
    III. The Attitude of Faith in Browne 51
    IV. His Tolerance 57
    V. Extent of His Skepticism 65
    VI. His Ethical Enlightenment and Opposition
       to Fanaticism 68

Chapter III. THE ART OF GOD
    I. Natural Philosophy in the Renaissance 77
    II. Browne's Philosophy of Nature in *Religio Medici* . 89

III. Providence and Fortune 105
IV. Spirit and Matter 112
V. Plastic Nature in *Vulgar Errors* 120
VI. Symbolism of *The Garden of Cyrus* 126

Chapter IV. THAT GREAT AMPHIBIUM

I. Seventeenth-Century Psychology 140
II. Browne's Psychology 146
III. The Theme of Mortality in Browne 155
IV. Contemporary Influences Affecting This Theme . . 161
V. Their Effect on Browne 170
VI. Conclusion 177

Index 179

Sir Thomas Browne

CHAPTER I

The World of Sir Thomas Browne

I

FOR the follower of intellectual byways in seventeenth-century England, no figure is more provocative and rewarding than Sir Thomas Browne. As antiquary, embryo naturalist, enlightened physician, restlessly speculative philosopher, he is an enduring personality whose name is inextricably woven into the age of Bacon, Gilbert, and Harvey. In the affairs of his day, through a long life which extended from the first year of James I to more than twenty years beyond the Restoration, he played a minor part, but with that brilliance and versatility which the impulses of the late Renaissance fostered so prolifically. He is one of the truest mirrors of that age, for he reflects in one direction its highest attainments and in another its most striking limitations. To the extent that he shares its superb genius for handling knowledge imaginatively he is one of its greatest men. As a deliberate artist, he seems, as far as literary judgment can predict, to have discovered that "antidote against the opium of time" whose existence he so magnificently despaired of. *Religio Medici* and *Urn Burial* and *The Garden of Cyrus* are now fixed stars, only less than the brightest in the English sky. But the astonishing genius of this writer is probably hidden from most of his readers, and those who have a primarily practical interest in the progress of exact knowledge will tend to regard his books mainly as a collection of scientific curiosities. Undoubtedly in this direction too they are a remarkable reflection of their time, for in Browne's pages we are carried back to that region of half-lights and uncertain ground in which the seventeenth century made its reluctant, groping transition from age-long modes of thought to the ruling conceptions of the modern world.

It was scarcely accidental that the unearthing of buried urns should inspire some of his most characteristic writing, for the urn philosophy wielded a subtle power over all his thought. The burial urn is his symbol for knowledge and for the world itself, and to many readers the connotation of the name Browne is probably most vividly suggested by that symbol. Seldom have a man and a word been more happily associated. "Time hath endless rarities," Browne wrote in the beginning of *Urn Burial*, "and shows of all varieties; which reveals old things in heaven, makes new discoveries in earth, and even earth itself a discovery. That great antiquity America lay buried for thousands of years, and a large part of the earth is still in the urn unto us." That Browne was no mere antiquary or quaint writer of prose meditations, but a man of active scientific curiosity and philosophic imagination, is well known; yet it is equally obvious that over all his writing is the pale cast of the medieval mind. And the quaint figure of the world in the urn unconsciously symbolizes this half-medieval approach to the new and revolutionary knowledge that was then being unearthed. It carries a realization that knowledge was buried treasure in the search for which the immense industry of all the past centuries had done little more than scratch the surface of the ground. But it suggests too that science is also in part an antiquarian process, the process of unearthing forgotten lore. In both these meanings it conveys the mood of the times.

The years of Sir Thomas Browne's life, from 1603 to 1682, saw greater changes, social, economic, political, religious, and scientific, than any comparable span of Western history. It has been said that "in 1600 the educated Englishman's mind and world were more than half medieval; by 1660 they were more than half modern."[1] This is true in science most of all, where the achieve-

[1] Douglas Bush, *English Literature in the Earlier Seventeenth Century—1600–1660* (Oxford, 1946), p. 1.

ments of the century were altogether revolutionary. Its genius lay in an unprecedented interest in direct observation. It had inherited, of course, from the Middle Ages logical discipline and the capacity for general principles. What was largely new and most fruitful was that it turned from deductive logic and *a priori* theories to an unprecedentedly close and patient observation of the "facts" of nature, to the process of weighing and measuring, reviving for the first time since the Greeks a speculative and skeptical interest in the "real" nature of things. It produced the ruling conceptions and methods of modern science and made major discoveries in many fields.

The effect of this upon traditional beliefs is too familiar to need discussion. The world-view of historic Christianity, with its harmonious and complete globe of knowledge, its criteria, its values, its conceptions of God, nature, and man, was undermined. The historic theology had been on the defensive for some time, but the cumulative pressure of new discoveries, especially in astronomy, was decisive and before the end of the century the physical sciences had assumed the pre-eminent place in thought and practical life that they have held ever since.

The sudden and revolutionary character of the new science, for those who thought about it, brought mixed feelings. For some there was delight in the contemplation of the enlarging universe, and there was optimism and hope of progress in the Baconian program for the conquest of nature, with its glittering slogan, "Knowledge is power"; others, gazing at the face of an unrecognizable cosmography, were filled with fear, or melancholy, or skepticism, or even despair, feeling that with the passing of the harmony and order of the old world-view man had lost his spiritual home.

It is no part of our business here to weigh the gains and losses of the seventeenth century. The gains of course were immense both in new knowledge and eventual material progress. In the general opinion of the eighteenth century these gains were almost unalloyed, and the doubts of the nineteenth failed to quench the prevailing optimism. The mid-twentieth century, with its profound disillusionments and uncertainties, surveys the road of progress with less complacency. And as for science itself, it is once more making discoveries so revolutionary that, as in the seventeenth century, they are beyond the grasp of the common man and scarcely a part of his philosophy. But the indications are that first principles are once more being re-examined, and that metaphysics, far from being dead, is re-entering the scene by way of the physicist's laboratory. It is clearer than at any time in the past that modern science is in need of a general, unifying philosophy, and that its achievements have necessarily been partial and narrow. To put it more emotionally, scientific materialism has never seemed less true, or less able to satisfy the spirit of man. The expression of such an attitude is not out of place here, for it is necessary to suggest at the outset that the history of seventeenth-century religious philosophy is not merely the history of exploded notions.

It was the incompatible mixture of old and new elements that gave the seventeenth century its unique character. It announced the rejection of Aristotle's binding authority, but for some decades, as the shortcomings of Bacon's perplexing philosophy so thoroughly demonstrate, it was really shackled by it. Exploration had outrun method, a few luminous minds had discovered new principles whose far-reaching consequences were but half anticipated even by themselves, to say nothing of scientific camp followers, chance experiment had borne strange fruit, and, not least enticing, the occult sciences with a last burst of vitality had budded once more into a kind of dying efflorescence.

For the average man it was a world of traveler's tales and disquieting rumors about the movement of the planets. All but the few greatest minds were sailing without chart or compass, and scientific interest took the form of a luxurious revelling in the rich and strange. Taine calls it the "floating and inventive curiosity" of the century. There is no better view of this than in the famous chapter on "Air Rectified" in Burton's *Anatomy*. Here Burton spreads out a crowded panorama of contemporary speculations about the earth, the sea, the air, and the heavens above, and touches it with irony and bizarre humor, as a part of his mad world. In this field, too, Browne furnishes the historian with some of his most richly fascinating documents. No one who wants to understand the seventeenth century should neglect to dip into *Vulgar Errors*. It is the twilight of the medieval gods. Here, as

THE WORLD OF SIR THOMAS BROWNE

through a gathering darkness, we see one of the last imposing processions of the great figures of old-world science — Aristotle, Galen, Hippocrates, Pliny, Augustine, Dioscorides, Bartholomew, Albertus Magnus. With a very learned and very naive admiration Browne sees the physical world through their eyes, and when he studies animals and plants and stars he enters their fairyland of monsters and prodigies and legendary tales and pious frauds. He has all their encyclopedic industry, all their credulity, all their lack of method, all their undisciplined curiosity.

Like Bacon he makes a list of idols, and points out the stultifying effects of credulity and adherence to authority, but his own views furnish the most picturesque illustrations of these very vices. He protests that he is "often constrained to stand alone against the strength of opinion, and to meet the Goliah and giant of authority with contemptible pebbles and feeble arguments, drawn from the scrip and slender stock of ourselves," [2] but in the role of David he is far too deferential to do much execution. Most of his "vulgar errors" are simply the venerable animal legends of the bestiaries, of Vincent of Beauvais and Bartholomew, but he reviews them so gravely and often parts with them so reluctantly as to leave the case much where he found it — in the endless circle of scholastic debate. He inherited those great weaknesses of the medieval logical method which Bacon analyzed so brilliantly; he breaks off a stick here and there instead of testing the strength of the whole faggot; he carries his candle into a corner and thereby darkens the room. He has a patristic reverence for the printed word which experiment can hardly shake, and natural history is still for him to a considerable extent a matter of research in a library, of citing and weighing authorities.

The result is that his birds and beasts sometimes have the fabulous air of never having lived outside of books. The hoary superstition that the salamander will live in fire is handled partly by deductive argument, partly by appealing from Aristotle, Nicander, and Pliny to Sextius, Dioscorides, Galen, Matthiolus, Scaliger, and other worthies, so that by the end of the chapter the little creature has been turned into a literary myth, a kind of phoenix, and the delightful error in question, though scotched,

[2] *Vulgar Errors,* "To the Reader."

is still able to drag itself into print, as it does a generation later in the records of the Royal Society.[3]

It might be supposed that Browne could have trapped a badger in England and by measuring it have disposed once for all of the legend that its legs are longer on the left side. But the text leaves us in doubt as to whether he had ever personally examined a badger. As usual, he prefers to cite authorities and evolve arguments on paper. "Albertus Magnus speaks dubiously, confessing he could not confirm the verity hereof; but Aldrovandus plainly affirmeth, there can be no such inequality observed. And for my own part, upon indifferent enquiry, I cannot discover this difference. . . . Again, it seems no easy affront unto reason, and generally repugnant unto the course of nature; for if we survey the total set of animals, we may in their legs, or organs of progression, observe an equality of length, and parity of numeration." [4]

We become so used to credulity in Browne that it is sometimes hard to know whether a given criticism of one of the ancients is meant for qualified praise or irony. He remarks of Oppianus that "abating the annual mutation of sexes in the hyæna, the single sex in the rhinoceros, the antipathy between two drums of a lamb and a wolf's skin, the informity of cubs, the venation of centaurs, the copulation of the murena and the viper, with some few others, he may be read with great delight and profit." [5] And, he continues, "it is not without some wonder his elegant lines are so neglected." This looks like a flash of dry humor, but the chances are that it is no such thing; for Browne's scientific world was still a wonderland, a strange mixture of fancy and fable, of persistent old legends and rumors of wonderful new tales brought home every month by travelers returned from foreign parts.

He revolves serenely in the old orbit that centered in the Ptolemaic astronomy and the cosmogony of Moses. Paracelsus, Cardan, and Joubertus stand on the frontier of knowledge and carry on the grand tradition. Except Harvey, contemporary scientists are given slight attention in *Vulgar Errors,* and though Copernicus, Galileo, Gilbert, and Descartes are mentioned with respect, they are not dignified to the level of authorities. He knew

---

[3] *Transactions of the Royal Society,* I, 377.
[4] *Vulgar Errors,* III, v.
[5] *Ibid.,* I, viii, 9.

vaguely that these men, like himself, were wandering "in the America and untraveled parts of truth," but he thought they could at most supplement ancient knowledge, and never dreamed that they would discover an utterly new world and set their backs forever on the old. In all this, however, he was not behind his age. *Vulgar Errors* is almost abreast of *Silva Silvarum* and the early publications of the Royal Society, and represents as well as they the average level of seventeenth-century science.

The fact is that Browne was an antiquary on a very large scale. Not only was he under the romantic spell of the past, but, intellectual aristocrat that he was, he stood like a Bourbon in the realm of philosophy and science on the proud vantage ground of a late, sophisticated age, conscious of its rich inheritance, and reluctant to admit any evidence of change. Once in a letter he had declared that Harvey's discovery was worth more than that of Columbus,[6] but later on in the preface to *The Garden of Cyrus* he refers to it in a tone almost of weary indifference, as though it were merely old knowledge already familiar to the omniscient past. "The field of knowledge," he writes placidly in those stormy days of 1658, "hath been so traced, it is hard to spring anything new. Of old things we write something new, if truth may receive addition, or envy will have anything new; since the ancients knew the late anatomical discoveries, and Hippocrates the circulation."

It is not that Browne lived chiefly in the past. He had an intense Renaissance interest in the present world, and an insatiable eagerness to keep abreast of scientific discovery. But like most men he failed to see the revolutionary significance of the changes that were going on about him; he thought of Gilbert's and Harvey's discoveries as important increments of knowledge, but as part of an unbroken tradition. It was natural, then, that the excitement of the time should produce in him frequent moods of world-weariness, and that he should fall back, as many did, on the renewed conviction that knowledge is vanity. And in these moods of intellectual exhaustion he felt that he was perhaps witnessing the last stages of a decaying and degenerating world. Science was buried knowledge, unearthed by accident in tiny frag-

[6] *Works*, VI, 277. (Wilkin [Bohn Library, 3 vols., 1852], III, 483; hereafter referred to simply as Wilkin.)

ments, almost too late for use, like the funeral urns of a dead civilization. He felt with something of ironic sadness the futility of attempting to dig up the treasures of a moldering old world, which were perhaps never to be revealed, no more to his day than to the venerable past. Knowledge was in the urn, the vessel that encloses mortal dust, and binds together past and present in the union of mortality.

So far as he embodies these traits Browne represents the typical limitations of his century. He is like a modern man walking on an enchanted island and subject to the potent sorcery of a magician. Scholasticism has not yet drowned its book or broken its staff, and whenever the intruder raises his arm this Prospero charms him from moving. To us who have a long perspective on the period the irresistible set of its current in the direction of eighteenth-century rationalism is easily perceptible, but very few of those who were caught in the mid stream of it knew where its swirling eddies were carrying them. Nowhere are the ebb and flow and cross currents of contemporary thought better shown than in the writings of Sir Thomas Browne, and certainly nowhere do we find a writer more richly endowed for conveying the most subtle and evanescent phases of that thought into literature. It is the many colored texture of a prose that weaves together the web of antique speculation, modern science, and romantic mysticism that has attracted generations of readers to his books, for they taste in them the precise flavor of that vanished age.

II

It was an extraordinary century. Put together a Bacon who could pull down the pillars of Aristotelianism but deny the Copernican theory, a Lord Herbert of Cherbury who could undermine the traditional belief in supernatural revelation in his *De Veritate,* and yet could pray for (and receive) a sign from heaven before publishing it, a Kenelm Digby who, although a member of the Royal Society, was advertising a powder of sympathy that cured from a distance, and reporting that burning glasses could gather light into a purple powder, a Boyle who was still looking for the philosopher's stone, a Newton who thought that God on occasion personally regulated minor irregularities of the solar system, a Puritan parliament which ordered the astrologers Lilly and Booker to attend the army at Colchester "to encourage the soldiers with predictions of speedy victory," a Royal Society whose conception of research did not exclude queries as to "whether diamonds and other precious stones grow again after three or four years in the same place where they have been digged out," or "what ground there may be for that relation concerning horns taking root and growing about Goa,"[7] — put all these together and *Vulgar Errors* seems no longer behind the times. The really solid achievements of science were soon to be tremendous in result, but as yet, in Browne's phrase, it was "an obscured virgin half out of the pit." Against this background Browne is not so extraordinary with his Paracelsian dream of a plant magically revived from its ashes, his lingering fondness for alchemy and astrology, his somber insistence that there are witches. It was an incongruous but a familiarly prevalent counterpart to the really scientific spirit that led him to dissect a dead whale on the Norfolk coast, and to watch germinating duckweed for hours together in the hope of detecting the first elemental stroke of the plant.

The scholastic philosophy had been shaken by the new astronomy and by Bacon's recent frontal assault but it was still largely in control. The *Speculum* of Vincent, or the *De Proprietatibus Rerum* of Bartholomew, with their grand hierarchy of life from mineral to angelic, constituted the accepted framework of thought. Science was not yet dehumanized, and nature was animate in all its parts, each endowed with its separate soul, and peopled with inhabiting spirits. Physical forces were in the picturesque and irrational control of demons and angels, and the control of nature was still thought of in terms of magic, of alchemy and astrology. Physicists and chemists were still looking for secret short cuts and magic formulas. To deny witchcraft was still regarded as close to atheism, for it cast doubt upon the devil and so upon all spiritual existence itself, and though a few

[7] Thomas Sprat, *History of the Royal Society of London* (1667), pp. 158, 161. The answer from Batavia to the question about horns was as follows: "Inquiring about this, a friend laughed, and told me it was a jeer put upon the Portuges, because the women of Goa are counted much given to lechery." The miraculous horns of Goa are also referred to in Browne's *Garden of Cyrus*, chap. iv.

doubters and scoffers like Montaigne, Selden, and Hobbes stood out against it, yet under the gloomy terrorism of the Catholic and Puritan regime alike women were burnt for witchcraft as late as 1680.

Physiology had scarcely made any progress since the days of the Greeks, for the rigid prohibition against the dissection of the human body had only just begun to be lifted. Only the most enlightened physicians had reached the point of abandoning their traditional dependence on astrology, and there was no great gap between the medical practitioner and the herbalist and distiller. The Cabbalist and Neo-Platonic speculations, if they were the esoteric and romantic fringe of philosophy, were nevertheless strong rivals of the orthodox system and constantly intermingled with it. Paracelsus was still a name to conjure with, and Dr. Dee, the alchemist, attracted more respect than ridicule. In many fields of experimentation scientists had not outgrown the notion, so firmly held by Browne, that they were practicing white magic, communicated by "the courteous revelations of spirits," or handed down from the black art of the devil's personal disciples.

There was as yet no thoroughgoing belief in the uniformity of nature, and the constant invasion of nature by the supernatural was taken as a matter of course. The time had scarcely come to study nature objectively and patiently. In the realm of experiment, the century had inherited too much of the theological rigidity, the impatience with novelty, the plodding, but timid and haphazard industriousness that had characterized the Middle Ages. "In trying to embrace what it could not seize dialectic only consolidated error. Unlike God, it made matter before light."[8] And though the conception of inflexible natural law was beginning to make headway, yet, as Thomas Huxley said, in discussing the crucial decade which saw the foundation of the Royal Society, large realms of happenings were not yet included in it; those who assigned causes for the double calamity of the fire and the plague attributed the former unhesitatingly to agents of the opposite political party, but agreed unanimously that the latter was the hand of God.

The most casual reader of Sir Thomas Browne at once feels himself in contact with a sensitive and powerful intellect which

[8] C. F. M. Rémusat, *Bacon*.

is creatively occupied with the ideas of its time. Here is the weight of classic authority, the blend of Greek, Christian, Jewish, and Hermetic philosophies, the strength of Galen, the fascination of Paracelsus, the romance of Bartholomew. But here too is the passion for research, the more than fugitive gleams of a new method, the dim promise of discovery that points to the future. He was incapable of the discipline of sustained scientific or philosophic thought, but he was no mere dabbler in floating curiosities. As a statement of the intellectual ideal there is nothing finer in the *Advancement of Learning* than the following passage:

"Let thy studies be free as thy thoughts and contemplations, but fly not only upon the wings of imagination; join sense unto reason, and experiment unto speculation, and so give life unto embryon truths, and verities yet in their chaos. There is nothing more acceptable unto the ingenious world, than this noble eluctation of truth; wherein, against the tenacity of prejudice and prescription, this century now prevaileth. . . . Who can but magnify the endeavors of Aristotle, and the noble start which learning had under him; or less than pity the slender progression made upon such advantages, while many centuries were lost in repetitions and transcriptions sealing up the book of knowledge? And therefore, rather than to swell the leaves of learning by fruitless repetitions, to sing the same song in all ages, nor adventure at essays beyond the attempt of others, many would be content that some would write like Helmont or Paracelsus; and be willing to endure the monstrosity of some opinions, for divers singular notions requiting such aberrations." [9]

But of course Browne's real genius lay in another region, in which the events and outward interests of his life become insignificant. That he was a country practitioner and amateur scientist is an accidental circumstance; he endures to fame as a literary artist, for as physician and naturalist he is always conscious of those

obstinate questionings
Of sense and outward things

which shape the artist's creative interpretation of life. He seemed to hold quiet communion with the spirit of nature, and as it re-

---

[9] *Christian Morals*, II, 5.

vealed itself to him, through the conceptions which he had inherited and the fresh disclosures of his own investigations, he was chiefly conscious of its deepening mystery, of the wonder of that "mystical mathematics" through which all things from smallest to greatest begin and end in order. By the determining bent of genius his imagination was most stimulated by the small objects in nature; in these he found "all Africa and her prodigies," and room for the farthest flights of speculation. These imaginative flights, as sudden as they are superb and daring, are among the chief poetic glories even of the age of Shakespeare and Milton. But brilliance in this field is as typical of the period as the scientific imagination of Bacon or Newton, and side by side with its genius for the statement of principles or for the discovery of exact knowledge ran that other lofty impulse of the Renaissance which found expression in Sir Thomas Browne.

To be sure there is something utterly solitary about this man's genius. He was not a social writer. "The world that I regard is myself," he said; "it is the microcosm of my own frame that I cast mine eye on; for the other, I use it but like my globe, and turn it round sometimes for my recreation." [10] He surrounds himself with an enchanted ring of subjective thought, or, perhaps better, he is a phoenix sprung from the ashes of old books. Coleridge truly remarks that "he reads nature neither by sun, moon, nor candle light, but by light of the faëry glory around his own head." He had friends enough, yet even in his own parish circle he probably had a reputation for a certain shy and saturnine reserve. Except for a few restrained passages in his letters, expressing abhorrence of "the abominable murder of King Charles the first" and his happiness at the Restoration, he so completely ignores the political situation that one might suppose the Puritan and turbulent Norwich to have been a happy island, completely cut off from the rest of England. By temperament he kept out of the political and philosophical storm centers throughout his career. One of the marked characteristics of *Vulgar Errors,* the one book of Browne which has a definite scientific aim, is its tendency to ignore or at least to pass lightly over contemporary names. The reader reaches the conviction that its author is too antiquated,

---

[10] *Religio Medici,* II, 11.

too cloistered, too much shut off from bracing conflicts to bring knowledge up to date.

And yet he was not a recluse. His books and, still more, his letters show that he was no mere dreamer or collector of curios in a romantic fairy land. *Religio Medici* is certainly something more than a subjective study of the paradoxes of metaphysical beliefs; it allies itself definitely and courageously with a religious party that was under double fire. The patristic obscurity of *Vulgar Errors* is illuminated by gleams of scientific insight and brilliant anticipations of later discoveries, and its criteria, however limited they may have been in application, are distinctly modern in spirit. Strangely enough *The Garden of Cyrus* is probably the most modern of all, for it reveals its author as a patient observer working with nature at first hand and at close range.

But Browne shows the range of his interests most clearly in his letters.[11] He was in active touch with men like Ashmole and Dugdale and Sir Hamon L'Estrange and Evelyn, some of them near neighbors, some well outside his provincial circle. He opened and maintained for years a correspondence with a certain Dr. Jonsson, an Icelandic scientist. He was the guide and mentor of a group of young medical students like Henry Power, later a fellow of the Royal Society, whom he inspired and encouraged with unflagging zeal. He followed eagerly the progress of continental medical science and the work of the teachers whom he had sat under in his youth. He read with assiduity the publications of the Royal Society, sent contributions and inquiries to Henry Oldenburg, its secretary, and may have cherished hopes of being elected to its membership.[12] Above all, as his son Edward rose to prominence as a fellow of the Royal Society, a professor in the Royal College of Physicians, and a fashionable prac-

[11] Our knowledge of this, especially as to his medical activities, has been enlarged by the new letters in the Keynes edition.

[12] Edward Browne had become a fellow of the Royal Society in 1667. In the next year he made a second tour of Europe, partly to collect specimens and information for the Royal Society. There is a series of letters of his in the library of the Royal Society, together with four letters to Oldenburg by Sir Thomas, who had acted as intermediary in the correspondence. Sir Edmund Gosse, who first discovered the latter, seems mistaken in saying (*Sir Thomas Browne* [New York, London, 1905], p. 150) that they show pique at being snubbed by Oldenburg.

titioner, he gave him constant and valuable counsel. Browne's circle of friends numbered men who were celebrities in their day, and through them he was in active contact with the contemporary intellectual life of England.

These, in rough outline, are the boundaries of Sir Thomas Browne's intellectual world. For the purposes of the study which is proposed here there is no need to fill in that outline. The facts of his life, so far as they are available, have been presented over and over again, and a review of them would serve no purpose. It is with more regret that we leave out of account his definitely scientific ideas. Yet here too there are consolations; for that inchoate mass of half-scholastic erudition which goes by the name of *Vulgar Errors* is largely a curiosity and a work of entertainment rather than instruction. Its prime quality is a quaintly romantic blend of science, fable, and flights of fancy which remains *sui generis*; so that perhaps the wisest criticism of it, as indeed the wisest reading, will be discursive. But before passing on, it may be worth while to glance at its critical principles, if only to bring into somewhat sharper focus what has already been said about Browne's general intellectual point of view.

Its author, who took himself with conscientious seriousness, observes by way of an apology for its fragmentary character that "a work of this nature is not to be performed upon one leg; and should smell of oil, if duly and deservedly handled." He would have been astonished and chagrined to find that oblivion has already scattered her poppy upon most of the revered volumes which he pored over beneath his midnight lamp, and that, as regards his contributions to knowledge, posterity, far from deploring his writing them upon one leg, reads them in the same manner.[13]

Vulgar Errors is one of those books that set us to dreaming on the shipwrecks of past intellectual voyages. Many of its ideas are noble hulls, many only the flotsam and jetsam of crude superstitions, Physiologus tales, semi-literary myths, learnedly ignorant

[13] Apparently even those who write about *Vulgar Errors* do not always read it through. If Sir Edmund Gosse, for instance, had done so he would not have blundered into the statement that Browne never once mentions Descartes in all his works (*op. cit.*, p. 37). Descartes is mentioned in II, ii; II, iii; and II, iv. But Bacon, Gilbert, and various other modern names are, of course, mere needles in the medieval haystack.

classical and scholastic scientific theories. Some are picturesque folklore, some pedantic queries known only to bookworms; some are inspired by tales of Elizabethan travelers; some are the elfish product of Browne's own fantastic mind. On the whole the errors which are exploited are learned rather than vulgar, and the author too often wastes his powder on dead enemies, on patristic debates and quibbles which had long ceased to interest first-class minds. In spite of the injection of some really acute biblical criticism, and some shrewd estimates of the shortcomings of medieval authorities, the book has that singular lack of contact with pioneer thought which was characteristic of most writing in the first half of the century. Curiously elaborated with immense learning, and illuminated with flashes of personal research, it is the mental output of a kind of blind Cyclops, or man of the cave — of a mind and a period which were unripe for such a work by some generations.

Apparently Bacon's passing recommendation that "a calendar of falsehoods and of popular errors now passing unargued in natural history" be undertaken supplied the hint for this work, and the long introductory analysis of the causes of human error is thoroughly Baconian, if not in analytical force at least in spirit. Error, says Browne, springs from the common infirmity of human nature, from the erroneous disposition of the people, from misapprehension, from credulity, from supinity, and from obstinate adherence to antiquity and authority. The proclamation of such principles has a certain ring of modernity and much of what is said about the obligation to extend the bounds of knowledge, though it is controlled by the theological doctrine that we can only "repair our primary ruins, and build ourselves men again," and with the medieval fear of unholy knowledge that comes "within command of the flaming swords," is, nevertheless, modern in spirit.

But in some respects, and this vastly enhances its charm, *Vulgar Errors* is an admirable example of subjection to the one class of idols which Bacon passes lightly over, the idols of the cave, for it is full of amazing fancies which no head but his could have conceived. And the broader limitations of the book become apparent in the final, climactic chapters of the introduction, which deals with "the last and common promoter of false opinions, the endeavors of Satan." Belief in the personal machinations of the devil is very real for Browne, and he shares with most of his contemporaries the patristic doctrine that the false angels set up shop on earth as heathen gods. Hooker adopts it and Milton makes dramatic use of it to invest his rebel angels with personality and link them pictorially with human history. Browne likewise makes Satan largely responsible for the whole development of ancient civilization. It is Satan who inspired the great rival schools of atheists, polytheists, and fatalists, and who also produced supernatural effects through oracles, magic, and divinations. Believing, as he so firmly does, that evil spirits are a necessary part of the scale of being and that their performances are very formidable, he draws a distinction between authentic and spurious miracles.[14] He does not deny that the devil has a superhuman command of natural forces; indeed he is inclined to think that even legitimate natural philosophy owes much of its knowledge to the black art. But his position is that although Satan can produce effects above nature by "secret and undiscerned ways," these are only counterfeit miracles, contrived by arranging effects to coincide with causes whose operation he can foresee; the oracularly commanded procedures by which pagan priests seemed to work cures were really irrational. When God, on the other hand, commanded seemingly irrational procedures phenomena actually became causes and produced supernatural effects, for, Browne argues, "he that hath determined their actions unto certain effects, hath not so emptied his own, but that he can make them effectual unto any other."

The great defect of such a point of view is its lack of historical imagination. But preconceptions such as those that underlie *Vulgar Errors* necessarily close the mind to any critical principles. Hooker had the imagination and philosophic breadth to discern that other religions contained some truth, and Cudworth began to see it still more clearly, but Cudworth himself devotes chapter after chapter to proving the theory, so dear to theologians then, that all the speculative truth of the ancient world derived originally from Moses. The conception of the universal evolution of knowledge could take no root until it was seen that the Bible

[14] *Vulgar Errors*, I, xi.

itself is an evolution. As long as implicit belief in the infallibility of Scripture guaranteed the scholastic science, with all its irrational mixture of natural and supernatural, of God and Satan, of science and magic, there could be no real knowledge either of the past or the present. Two things were needed: an epistemological science that would provide a workable theory of knowledge, and a consistent view of the behavior of nature. For lack of these principles *Vulgar Errors* is like Browne's debating babes in the womb: it is in constant danger of falling from a half truth into a whole absurdity.

With what eyes those brilliant and eager Renaissance scientists looked upon "the universal and public manuscript" of nature we can scarcely know without an act of imagination that effaces much of the story of the last three hundred years. Knowledge was indeed in the urn. In 1658 we find Dugdale writing to Browne for his theory about the fossils of trees and fish recently found near the coast. He had some notion that the region had once been under water, but of course only the vaguest inkling of the truth. "That which puzzles me most," he says, "is the sea coming up to Conington Downe."[15] Browne was musing over his urns at the time, speculating, among other things, upon the age of the charred pieces of wood that had been found in them, and as though he had been thinking of Dugdale's letter his mind turns for a comparison to the mysterious history of these buried trees — "the moor logs and fir trees found underground in many parts of England; the undated ruins of winds, floods, or earthquakes, and which in Flanders still show from what quarter they fell, as generally lying in a northeast position."

Again in 1660, puzzling over a large fish bone which Dugdale had sent, he suggests to him that it may be a relic of the Deluge. Some of the large fossils found in England, he thinks, might be the bones of elephants brought over by the Emperor Claudius.[16] With what incredulous astonishment he would have read Huxley's *Piece of Chalk*, and yet conceivably with what delight, too, as his imagination winged its way into the long nights of geologic time. But geology was a sealed chapter. Nature's book was still a black-letter manuscript.

[15] *Works*, VI, 348. (Wilkin, III, 500.)
[16] *Ibid.*, p. 348.

III

The subject of his connections with alchemy is an interesting one, but the existing evidence does not shed much light upon it. His books certainly betray no overweening interest in the matter, but he corresponded occasionally with a small circle of devotees.[17] We learn from his letters that he had been well acquainted with Arthur Dee, the son of the notorious Dr. John Dee, and for years a practicing physician in Norwich. On two occasions, evidently in reply to solicitations, he had sent Elias Ashmole, the author of the *Theatrum Chemicum,* detailed particulars about the writings and exploits of the elder Dee and some of his disciples.[18] The Earl of Yarmouth, Sir Robert Paston, also seems to have regarded Browne as a kindred spirit, for he wrote him excited descriptions of his experiments in transmutation.[19] And once in a letter to Edward, who was then traveling on the Continent, the elder Browne evinced a mild curiosity about the latest sensation of the kind. "When you were at Amsterdam," he writes, "I wish you had enquired after Dr. Helvetius, who writ *Vitulus Aureus,* and saw projection made, and had pieces of gold to shew of it." [20] This was in 1668, the year after Dr. John Frederick Helvetius had published a romantic and circumstantial account of his conversion to alchemy upon being secretly visited by a grave stranger and presented with a lump of the "medicine." [21] But beyond a few stray facts of this sort, which show at most a detached interest, there is nothing to build on. If Browne was indeed an enthusiast he kept his secret well.

It has sometimes been conjectured, however, that he had enough of a reputation as an alchemist to debar him from a distinction which he seems to have coveted, and for which he might otherwise have been qualified — namely, membership in the Royal Society. But had the Royal Society really outgrown alchemy? Bishop Sprat, to be sure, refers with irritation to the hopeless obsessions of the alchemists — "downright enthusiasts" he calls

---

[17] Gosse (pp. 135 ff.) seems to describe Browne's part in this with a higher color of detail than the available facts warrant.

[18] *Works,* VI, 324, 327. (Wilkin, III, 516, 530.)

[19] Wilkin, III, 513, 514.

[20] *Works,* VI, 34. (Wilkin, III, 428.)

[21] This interesting story is told at length in Arthur Waite's *Lives of Alchemystical Philosophers* (London, 1888).

them, who are unable to see an inch to the right or left of their quest.[22] "And," he continues, "seeing we cast enthusiasm out of divinity itself, we shall hardly sure be persuaded to admit it into philosophy." If only these men were sober chemists, and did not expect "to gain the Indies out of every crucible, there might be wonderful things expected of them" — such things, he declares, as some of the society's chemists were actually achieving abroad. Had alchemy been already an outcast science, such a position would be thoroughly understandable. But when we remember the exploits of Digby and Glanvill, both saturated in all manner of occult beliefs and both active members of the society, to say nothing of Boyle himself, it becomes clear that such was not the case. Alchemy was certainly not altogether dead.

It is difficult, in fact, to say what alchemy really was. The mere transmutation of baser metals was no longer especially alluring. The science had long since been metamorphosed into a search for the elixir of life and magical remedies for disease, and its devotees, many of them followers of Paracelsus, interpreted chemical processes in terms of the "cosmic spirit," and the mystical sympathies and antipathies between nature and man. It had passed into a full-fledged mystical cult of purification, contemplation, and self-discipline, and in this form was simply an inchoate, nebulous part of religious knowledge.

Ashmole's fantastic book is a typical embodiment of this surviving mixture of magic and religion. He pretends that he is returning to the ideas of the ancient Hermetic philosophers, to whom gold was primarily precious as the symbol of wisdom: "And certainly he to whom the whole course of nature lies open rejoiceth not so much that he can make gold and silver or the devils to become subject to him, as that he sees the heavens open, the angels of God ascending and descending and that his own name is fairly written in the book of life." We learn here no vulgar secrets as to the nature of the prima materia, that "bird of Jove," or "Virgin's son," nor as to how the magnum opus was effected. If Ashmole knows any he disdains to divulge them, though he declares of a certain marvelous operation that "this as E. A. assures you is not any ways necromantical, or devilish, but easy, wondrous easy, natural and honest." There are four

[22] *Op. cit.*, pp. 37 ff.

stones, the mineral, vegetable, magical, and angelical, of which only the first transmutes metals, and the others are so increasingly subtle that the highest, the angelical, is sublimated into an incorporeal something that resembles the mystical body in the holy wafer. This is so subtle, Ashmole says, that it cannot be seen, felt, or weighed, but tasted only. It is called the food of angels, the tree of life. Only Moses, Solomon, and Hermes were masters of it, and its possessor, it is said, cannot die, although it brings such revelations that he would long to be at once dissolved into their full fruition. How extensive the practice of this Hermetic mysticism was, or how wide were its ramifications it would be difficult to determine, but obviously its devotees were a kind of esoteric priests and their crucible had become a religious symbol.

On the other hand, alchemy was emerging into chemistry, into a search for physical elements, for a means of breaking down compounds into their structural principles and so unlocking nature's powers. Ashmole represents this side of it as well. He protests angrily that alchemy is not vulgar magic; it is rather "applying agents to patients" in order to search into the hidden virtues of nature. Witches he calls "those grand impostors, who violently intrude themselves into magic, as if swine should enter into a fair and delicate garden and (being in league with the Devil) make use of his assistance in their works, to counterfeit and corrupt the admirable wisdom of the magi, between whom there is as large a difference as between angels and Devils." He insists that alchemy is that comprehensive science which "reduces all natural philosophy from the variety of speculations to the magnitude of works, and whose mysteries are far greater than the natural philosophy now in use and reputation will reach unto. For by the bare application of actives to passives it is able to exercise a kind of empire over nature and work wonders." Not only is this reminiscent of the vocabulary of Browne,[23] but to some extent of Bacon. It has to be kept in mind that the control of nature was still thought of in terms of occult formulas, and that the chemistry of Boyle and van Helmont had its roots in these very ideas, and is not to be disentangled from them.

If Browne can be called an alchemist it is only in the vague sense that he loved most the fanciful and romantic side of chem-

[23] Cf. *Vulgar Errors*, I, xi; *Religio Medici* uses the same analogy (I, 31).

istry. He was interested in it, as in every other science, largely from the mystical point of view, and he seldom pushed far in any other direction. Perhaps the key to his whole philosophy is an early sentence in *Religio Medici*: "The severe schools shall never laugh me out of the philosophy of Hermes, that this visible world is but a picture of the invisible, wherein, as in a portrait, things are not truly, but in equivocal shapes, and as they counterfeit some more real substance in that invisible fabric." [24] It is these "equivocal shapes" that constantly absorb his attention, and he draws from them a wealth of analogies and symbols to support his doctrines of the creation of the material world, of the nature of angels, of the resurrection of the body, and a multitude of other mystical truths. For the most part, considering the intoxicating draughts of mysticism which his reading must have supplied, he exercises a considerable artistic restraint. Once, it is true, in the search for a symbol of the resurrection he rashly states that Paracelsus' feat of restoring a plant out of its ashes is possible.[25] But usually the symbolism is handled with reserve. Thus, on the union of soul and body, he writes, "The smattering I have of the philosopher's stone (which is something more than the perfect exaltation of gold) hath taught me a great deal of divinity, and instructed my belief, how that immortal spirit and incorruptible substance of my soul may lie obscure, and sleep awhile within this house of flesh." [26] So again he says of the dwelling place of angels, "Do but extract from the corpulency of bodies, or resolve things beyond their first matter, and you discover the habitation of angels." [27] Or again, on the mystical indwelling of the divine presence: "There is a common spirit that plays within us, yet makes no part of us; and that is, the spirit of God, the fire and scintillation of that noble and mighty essence, which is the life and radical heat of spirits, and those essences that know not the virtue of the sun. . . . This is that gentle heat that brooded on the waters, and in six days hatched the world." [28] In all this we have the familiar terms and conceptions of the al-

[24] *Religio Medici*, I, 12.
[25] *Ibid.*, I, 48. Cf. William Drummond, *A Cypress Grove* (The Muse's Library), p. 281.
[26] *Ibid.*, I, 39.
[27] *Ibid.*, I, 35.
[28] *Ibid.*, I, 32.

chemists; but in passing through Browne's mind they have suffered a delicate sea-change. They have been stripped of extravagance, and are transfigured by a lofty, an almost austere imagination.

One concludes in his case that it was not so much any definite connection with alchemy as the whole transcendental bent of his mind that would have put the Royal Society on its guard. The society was beginning to search for facts in the modern way, and it was determined to cut itself free from the old meshes of metaphysics, from the aimless medieval search for prodigies and wonders, from the vices of rhetoric. Sprat has illuminating things to say about all these matters. The ideals of the society, he says, had actuated it to ban works on God and the soul, or any phase of psychology, for fear "that if such discourses should be once entertained, they would be in danger of falling into talking instead of working." [29] Later on, when natural science had advanced sufficiently, it might be possible to throw new light on these subjects, but for the present they were to be avoided. He goes on to contrast the ancient natural historians, who collected tales of prodigies, of wonderful gems, of rarities in beasts and minerals and fountains and rivers, with the present sober naturalists, and remarks dryly that "it is like romance in respect of true history." Finally he has a furious passage on the demoralizing effects of rhetoric, of eloquence, of figures of speech.[30] In his opinion most arts and professions are already overgrown with this rank vegetation. The Royal Society had to keep the strictest guard lest "the whole spirit and vigor of their design had been soon eaten out by the luxury and redundance of speech." What they demanded of their writers above all else was that they "bring all things as near the mathematical plainness as they can." The honest, bluff English of artisans was to be preferred to that of wits and scholars, and he predicts that if England is to lead the world in experimental knowledge, as he believes she soon will, the prime factor in that progress will be her genius for practical, straightforward thinking.

In all these strictures, of course, he puts his finger on the sali-

[29] *Op. cit.*, p. 82.
[30] *Ibid.*, pp. 111 ff.

ent characteristics of Browne's temperament and literary style. Perhaps the difference between Edward Browne and his father provides us with the proper criterion. The son, unimaginative and keenly practical, seems to belong to a different world. He had none of his father's greater gifts, but he had inherited his keen mind and his strong bent for medical research, and it carried him to success and distinction. He had begun to examine his world under the dry light of reason, in the spirit of the rising generation.

It is unfortunate that the one event in Browne's life which posterity has chosen to remember vividly is the picturesque but sinister circumstance that he was present at a witch trial at Bury St. Edmunds in 1664, when two wretched women were on trial for their lives, and added his testimony to the evidence on which they were condemned. The incident is doubly regrettable in that it is the one possible blot on a singularly blameless record, and, besides, has the melancholy distinction of being almost the last chapter in the long, dark history of a barbarous superstition. Curiously, or perhaps quite naturally, this now celebrated witch trial attracted no contemporary notice whatever, and the record of it was unearthed only after all the participants had left the stage. What unkindly train of circumstances led Thomas Browne into the court room where Sir Matthew Hale was sternly presiding over this judicial murder we have no means of knowing, but the memory of that day in Suffolk has been obstinately persistent. It is the one circumstance of his life for which his admirers have to offer any apologies.

There is no denying that Browne's part in this sorry business was a blunder, but until recently even the friendliest critics have made it appear more tragic than it really was, simply because they ignored the one obviously authentic and complete account of the trial, although it was all the while easily available, and depended on a misleading secondary source. Some years ago a contributor to *Notes and Queries* [31] called attention to the interesting fact that a full account of the trial [32] by a court reporter present at

[31] Malcolm Letts, "Sir Thomas Browne and Witchcraft," *Notes and Queries*, 11th ser., Vol. V (March 23, 1912), 221–23.
[32] *A Tryal of Witches, at the assizes held at Bury St. Edmunds, etc. . . . Taken by a Person then Attending the Court* (London, 1682).

the proceedings appears in Cobbett and Howell's *State Trials*,[33] and that it differs in important respects from the source that Browne's biographers had relied on. This neglected document, as the aforesaid article pointed out, puts quite a new construction upon Browne's part in the trial.[34] The whole matter is interesting enough to be reviewed with some care.

The accepted view had been that Browne played a decisive part in the trial. The story was that on March 1, 1664, he had sat through the trial of two old women of Suffolk, Amy Duny and Rose Cullender, at Bury St. Edmunds, before the famous Sir Matthew Hale; that finally the evidence was all in and the case ready for the jury; that Hale, however, was extremely dubious about the value of the testimony, and so uncertain in his mind that he hesitated to charge the jury; that in his perplexity he appealed to Browne for his opinion; that at this juncture the latter, when the lives of the accused were at stake, turned the tide against them by declaring that the plaintiffs were unquestionably bewitched and that witchcraft was possible; and that this opinion so influenced both judge and jury as to bring about the conviction and the death sentence which followed.

This view seems to have been based exclusively on the Rev. Francis Hutchinson's *Historical Essay,* a famous attack on witchcraft published in 1718, which practically put an end to the superstition. It is an able argument, in the form of a debate between a liberal clergyman and a credulous defender of the old superstitious beliefs, but though it analyzes the evidence presented in a number of famous witch trials, that of Bury St. Edmunds among them, it does not give an orderly account of the actual procedure in any case, and the critical student of witch trials who wants to know just what happened in court finds this *Essay* very unsatisfactory.

This is particularly true of the case in question, and here it

[33] William Cobbett, T. B. Howell, comps., *A Complete Collection of State Trials and Proceedings for High Treason . . . from the Earliest Period to the Year 1783* (London, 1816–26), VI, 647–702.

[34] There is a full analysis of the Cobbett and Howell report in Wallace Notestein, *A History of Witchcraft in England from 1558 to 1718* (Washington: The American Historical Association, 1911), as well as an illuminating discussion of Sir Thomas Browne and Sir Matthew Hale. Dorothy Tyler has reviewed this whole matter in *Anglia* LIV (1930), 179–95.

happens that Hutchinson's method is responsible for a serious misinterpretation of the situation. Because Hutchinson regarded Browne's testimony as the climax of stupidity in this dismal affair and so treated it, the reader is allowed to gather the impression that it was actually given at the close of the trial. In his biography, Sir Edmund Gosse, who depended on Hutchinson, evidently so interpreted the facts, for he plays up the scene very strongly, representing that Hale turned to Browne as a last resource, that the court was against the prosecution, and that a single favorable word or even silence would have saved the women's lives. As a matter of fact, however, this version of the story seems to be entirely wrong. The Cobbett and Howell report is none too coherent, but it distinctly implies that Browne made his declaration not at the end, but in the middle of the trial, before the last three witnesses, out of the eleven called, had given their testimony, and before the series of tests demanded by Sergeant Keeling and other skeptical onlookers had completely exposed the farcical absurdity of the evidence. The truth seems to be that after Browne's remarks, noncommittal at best, the trial broke down completely; the tests for fraud were so conclusive, and the testimony of the remaining witnesses so scandalously worthless that only a judge and jury blinded by the grossest superstition could have concurred in a sentence. It was in the face of all this that the judge solemnly quoted Scripture to support his belief in witchcraft, and the jury returned a verdict of guilty within half an hour. Looked at in its proper setting the effect of Browne's declaration was really very insignificant, for, judging by what we know of the psychology of witch scares in Puritan England and the character and opinions of Sir Matthew Hale, the fate of the miserable women was almost sealed before the trial began.

As a sidelight upon perhaps the most extraordinary aspect of English life in the seventeenth century this old record has unusual interest. The owner of the manuscript, who got it at second hand, was impelled in the year 1682 to put it into print, partly because it seemed to be "the most perfect narrative of anything of this nature hitherto extant," partly because of its connection with Sir Matthew Hale. The fact that this eminent juror not only had given the case his closest attention but had had the assistance of "several other very eminent and learned persons" was felt to make it a kind of test case.

It is certainly a melancholy, but an all too typical story. Two old women had been accused of bewitching several children. The testimony of their parents and neighbors as recorded was thoroughly irrational and contradictory, and dealt with events of from five to seven years' standing. Amy Duny, it seems, had suckled one of the children against orders; the mother quarreled with her, and the child soon after fell sick. The mother, with characteristic inconsistency, had called in a witch doctor and under his instructions found damning proof of witchcraft in the shape of a toad which she had exorcised out of the child's blanket, and which when thrown into the fire exploded like gunpowder. The next day it was reported that Amy had been found to be mysteriously scorched with fire from head to foot. Apparently this was a type of evidence that a seventeenth-century court accepted so implicitly that cross-examination would never have been dreamed of. Then followed the usual stories of spasms and apparitions and of vomiting nails and crooked pins. According to the testimony of several other persons, seven in all, various other children had been similarly afflicted. It transpired that some months earlier the women had been searched for bodily marks. This was one of the most revolting but commonest methods of proving traffic with Satan, and in the famous Lancashire case of 1635 Harvey himself had found such a mark on an accused woman. In the present instance the examiners had discovered the expected mark on Rose Cullender.

After these eight witnesses had been heard several barristers of more or less reputation who were present, especially Sergeant Keeling, protested that, admitting the children were bewitched, the evidence was entirely insufficient to convict the prisoners. It was at this point that Browne was invited to give an opinion. His appearance upon the scene is recorded as follows: "There was also Dr. Brown of Norwich, a person of great knowledge; who after this evidence given, and upon view of the three persons in court, was desired to give his opinion, what he did conceive of them: and he was clearly of opinion, that the persons were bewitched; and said, that in Denmark there had been lately a great discovery of witches, who used the very same way of afflicting persons, by conveying pins into them, and crooked as these pins were, with needles and nails. And his opinion was, that the devil in such cases did work upon the bodies of men and women, upon a natural foundation, (that is) to stir up, and excite such humors superabounding in their bodies to a great excess, whereby he did in an extraordinary manner afflict them with such distempers as their bodies were most subject to, as particularly appeared in these children; for he conceived, that these swooning fits were natural, and nothing else but that they call the mother, but only heightened to a great excess by the subtlety of the devil, cooperating with the malice of these which we term witches, at whose instance he doth these villainies."

But evidently these remarks, however they may have chimed with the views of the court, made little impression on others. During the trial the prosecution had scored heavily by demonstrating that the children, who seemed to be in intermittent fits of stupor or convulsions, could suddenly be brought shrieking out of them by the mere touch of the accused women. This was mightily impressive. It was suggested, however, that to guard against counterfeiting it might be well to blindfold the children and see whether they could really distinguish the witches' touch from any one else's. Hale accordingly appointed a committee to make such a test. The result of course was that the blindfolded child immediately guessed wrong and shrieked at the touch of the first bystander, and the examiners reported that the whole transaction was a fraud. We are told that "this put the Court and all persons into a stand." Their perplexity, however, was short-lived, for Mr. Pacy, the father of two of the children, and one of the principal witnesses, made the astonishing suggestion "that possibly the maid might be deceived by a suspicion that the witch touched her when she did not," and this naively oracular remark was allowed to be a valid answer to the doubters.

In the face of a frenzied public opinion it is apparent that nothing could have saved the women. The remaining evidence should have been laughed out of court. One ignorant and evidently malicious fellow testified that Rose Cullender had once bewitched a cart which he was driving to the harvest field because it had damaged her window in passing, so that it had later stuck fast and had to be unloaded at a distance from his house, and those who helped him worked so hard that their noses bled and they gave up until morning. Evidently the woman had a sharp tongue, and he had harbored a longstanding grudge against her for berating his drunken or clumsy driver. Another man, curiously enough, had exasperated her by doing precisely the same thing, and he testified that after the accident he had suffered a continued series of disasters and sickness. Finally a woman told an incoherent story to the effect that Amy Duny had once made her lose a firkin of herrings by bewitching it out of the boat as the sailors were bringing it to shore. Having been allowed to introduce the slanderous gossip of these wretched villagers, the state rested its case.

Upon the conclusion of the evidence, Hale proceeded to charge the jury. He contented himself with reminding them "that they had two things to enquire after. First, Whether or no these children were bewitched? Secondly, Whether the prisoners at the bar were guilty of it?" He had no doubt, he said, that there were witches, for the Scriptures had affirmed it, and all nations had legislated against it. Sternly invoking divine guidance in this particular case, he charged them to judge according to the evidence. In half an hour a verdict of guilty was brought in and the accused were sentenced to death. To the admiration of the whole village the children were immediately cured of their ailments. The sentence was carried out within the month.

It is somewhat singular that this case attracted no contemporary notice. There is no mention of it in Bishop Burnet's *Life of Hale*, and none of Browne's early biographers make any allusion to it. The Lord Chief Justice had an immense prestige, being considered "on all hands to be the most profound lawyer of his time," and the fact that, so far as we are aware, this was the only case of the kind with which he was ever connected, and the further circumstance that such trials were becoming more and more rare makes the silence still more peculiar. It is not likely that the friends either of Hale or Browne were ashamed of it, and in any event it was not done in a corner, and must have exerted no little influence on subsequent witch trials. However that may be, the fact remains that Browne played a relatively unimportant role in the affair and that the responsibility rests squarely upon Hale.

This becomes doubly clear when it is remembered that Hale

was a close friend of Baxter, who believed unalterably in witchcraft, that he had read Henry More and probably accepted the general doctrine, as of course Browne did, that to deny witches overthrows the spiritual hierarchy, and that, finally, he had been a Puritan and had grounded his beliefs and principles on the Puritan view of the Bible. It was said of him in connection with this trial that "the rectitude of his intentions while under the strong bias of strong prejudices, might sometimes betray him into great mistake." [35] Evidently the subject of witchcraft was one of his harshest prejudices and on this occasion he judged sternly according to his religious lights. If Browne influenced him at all, it was only in the direction of that inflexible prejudice.

Browne's own general views on witchcraft had been expressed long before. To deny it seemed to him little short of atheism, for the scale of spiritual creatures depended on the existence of the devil, and the devil's legitimate medium of operation was the willing cooperation of those who were in league with him. Since the cessation of oracles he could work only through the contemptibly imperfect powers of these creatures. "It is a riddle to me," he had said many years before, "how this story of oracles hath not wormed out of the world that doubtful conceit of spirits and witches; how so many learned heads should so far forget their metaphysics, and destroy the ladder and scale of creatures, as to question the existence of spirits. For my part, I have ever believed, and do now know, that there are witches: they that doubt of these, do not only deny them, but spirits; and are obliquely, and upon consequence, a sort not of infidels, but atheists. Those that to confute their incredulity desire to see apparitions, shall questionless never behold any, nor have the power to be so much as witches; the devil hath them already in a heresy as capital as witchcraft; and to appear to them, were but to convert them." [36] To inspire unbelief in this matter, in other words, was the devil's masterstroke.

Browne believes likewise in changelings, and that the devils can "assume, steal, or contrive a body" and so have a certain feeble carnal connection with human beings, yet he insists that they can operate only through such a medium, and he is inclined

[35] Foster's preface, noted in Cobbett and Howell, VI, 647.
[36] *Religio Medici*, I, 30.

to be cautious in the matter of devil possession. "I hold that the devil doth really possess some men, the spirit of melancholy others, the spirit of delusion others." There is, that is to say, no satanic possession without willing cooperation.

His later remarks on witchcraft only repeat these convictions. He says again in *Vulgar Errors* that when the devil wants to lead men into denying his existence "he endeavors to propagate the unbelief of witches, whose concession infers his coexistency; by this means also he advanceth the opinion of total death, and staggereth the immortality of the soul; for, such as deny there are spirits subsistent without bodies, will with more difficulty affirm the separated existence of their own." [37]

And yet there is a certain cool-headedness about all this which reminds us of the attitude of such half-skeptics as Bacon and Harvey. Intelligent men already regarded magic and witchcraft with unmixed contempt, recognizing that at most their effects were decidedly feeble. In this spirit Browne derides the plight of the devil, in that "expelled from oracles and solemn temples of delusion, he runs into corners, exercising minor trumperies, and acting his deceits in witches, magicians, diviners, and such inferior seducers," [38] and he rebukes those who rely on their feeble and usually spurious powers: "In vain we cry that oracles are down; Apollo's altar still doth smoke; nor is the fire of Delphos out unto this day." [39]

In the light of these views his remarks at Bury St. Edmunds are what we should expect. He expressed no opinion, it is to be observed, about the guilt of the accused, but he was satisfied that the children were bewitched, and that witchcraft consisted simply in the power of certain persons in league with the devil to aggravate natural disorders. The citation of recent cases in Denmark is almost startlingly lifelike; it reminds us vividly and amusingly that this is none other than the bookish author of *Vulgar Errors*. But the situation was not amusing, and Hutchinson quite justly excoriates Browne for condemning the accused women out of a book. One wonders what these cases in Denmark

[37] *Vulgar Errors*, I, x.
[38] *Ibid.*, VII, xii.
[39] *Ibid.*

could have been. Hutchinson says that four women had been burnt at Kjöge, in Zealand, two years before, but that Bekker had disposed of the case against them. The book referred to is a quaint attack on witchcraft, not published, however, until 1695, entitled *The World Bewitched*, by Balthazar Bekker, a Dutch clergyman, who was driven out of the church for writing it. We find there the story of the women burned at Kjöge, but it had happened long before, in 1601 and 1602, and there is no other mention of witchcraft in Denmark. Like many another of Browne's allusions, this one to witches in Denmark must probably remain a myth.

Equally mysterious is the source of his insistent statement in *Religio Medici*, "I do now know that there are witches." The only cases of any importance between 1633 and 1645 were the famous Lancashire trials of 1633[40] with which Harvey was connected, and it is of course possible that he found in that wild scare evidence enough to turn his faith into knowledge. It is interesting to note that the published catalogue of his library seems to contain only one work on witchcraft, "The opinion of witchcraft vindicated in an answer to a book Intitled The Question of Witchcraft Debated. Being a letter to a Friend. By R. T. 1670."

It would be pleasant to turn biographer in earnest and attempt a fuller description of the life and times of Sir Thomas Browne. We have dwelt at length on a single day at Bury St. Edmunds when for once he stepped into the harsh light of public affairs. To do him justice we ought to turn to the normal events of his life at Norwich, where he was loved and venerated for long years as friend and physician and distinguished citizen, where he brought up his large and attractive family of children, where he tended his garden and collected his specimens of plants and birds and beasts, and pored over his books. Here Evelyn came to see him, and here on a royal progress King Charles II, as elegant patron of science, conferred knighthood upon him.

One other event, the mysterious and ironic fate that befell Browne's remains in the church of St. Peter Mancroft, may be mentioned. It is well known that he detested the desecration of dead bodies. "To be gnawed out of our graves, to have our skulls

[40] See Wallace Notestein, *op. cit.*, for this interesting case.

made drinking bowls and our bodies turned into pipes . . . are tragical abominations escaped by burning burials." [41] It was his uncanny fate to have his skull "gnawed" out of his grave and exhibited in the hospital museum at Norwich from the late 1840's until recent years. The culprit originally responsible for this outrage was probably a local antiquary, but the whole affair is involved in mystery, and there has even been some doubt as to the identity of the skull, which is unexpectedly low-browed. Most of the portraits of Browne are uncertain likenesses, but the two which are regarded as most trustworthy, known as the L'Estrange portrait and the Buccleuch miniature, seem to confirm the identity of the skull.[42]

In July 1922, the skull was reinterred in the wall of the chancel, with the following inscription by the Bishop of Norwich —

> O caput augustam, Petro custode sepulcri
> Sit tibi pax; nomen vivat in urbe; vale.

All in all the recorded glimpses of Browne's life are few and fleeting, and for us he lives in the world of thought rather than of men and affairs. His books reveal how rich and deep was the vein of that thought. It is in them, with their breadth of charity, their metaphysical sweep, their deep understanding of the medieval world, their ardent perception of the mystery of life, that what has endured of him finds its continuing projection.

IV

The aim of the present study is to expand as fully as may be the phrases just employed, to attempt to explain some of the philosophical conceptions of these books, to trace their historic antecedents, and to set them against the background of contemporary modes of thought. Such a study, however, is not to be undertaken without considerable hesitation. For one thing, the subject is difficult, perhaps too difficult for a lay philosopher; and, besides, to be merely pedestrian or ponderous would be fatal. Browne is certainly not to be systematized, and he has no impor-

---

[41] *Urn Burial*, chap. iii.
[42] See M. L. Tildesley, "Sir Thomas Browne: His Skull, Portraits, and Ancestry," *Biometrika*, XV (1923), 1–76; also the article in the *British Medical Journal*, May 6, 1922, by the Rev. Canon F. J. Meyrick, Vicar of St. Peter Mancroft.

tant place in the line of English thought, and ought not to be weighed in the same scales with Hooker, or Bacon, or Cudworth. Accordingly such a writer as Tulloch[43] when he studies English religious thought in the seventeenth century quite properly dismisses Browne in a few words, merely grouping him with a number of minor writers who deserve bare mention in his final summary. And not long ago Lytton Strachey,[44] after commending Gosse for attempting nothing more than an informal and desultory criticism, proceeded to follow his example, on the principle that Browne is primarily a man of letters and should be studied chiefly from the literary point of view. This of course has been the method of Hazlitt, Leslie Stephen, and Pater, in fact of all the best-known interpreters of Sir Thomas Browne, and they have done full justice to his qualities as an artist. Remembering all this, one may well hesitate to lay a heavy and unskillful hand upon *Religio Medici* or *The Garden of Cyrus*.

Yet it is obvious to anyone who reads him that Browne's world is the world of metaphysical conceptions, and it is equally obvious that these have surpassing beauty and often original intellectual force. In his own day, of course, his philosophical ideas excited attention. *Religio Medici* had considerable fame as a vigorous and daring piece of speculation, as is readily apparent from its history. The interesting story of Sir Kenelm Digby's delighted discovery of the pirated edition, and his discriminating *Observations* that forced Browne to acknowledge and print the book, the successive translations into various languages, always with the notice of savants in France and Germany and elsewhere, the floating comments for years as to its religious views, the stamp of "haereticus" on at least one edition, and the compliment of a place in the Index all point to the conclusion that Browne had fame as a religious thinker. *Vulgar Errors*, museum piece though it now is, went into six editions within Browne's lifetime and was translated into four foreign languages. Browne's books are great for many reasons, not the least of which is that they are a record of ideas, and notwithstanding the fact that he has been the subject of some of the most charming essays in English criti-

[43] John Tulloch, *Rational Theology and Christian Philosophy in England in the Seventeenth Century* (Edinburgh, 1872).
[44] In *Books and Characters* (London, 1922).

cism, many of them by famous writers, and has had the advantage of the finest editorial scholarship, there remain perhaps considerable tracts of unexplored territory, or, as Browne himself modestly says at the beginning of a famous peroration, "a large field is yet left unto sharper discerners to enlarge upon this order."

CHAPTER II

Faith and Reason

I

As a writer about religion Sir Thomas Browne stands in luminous and winning contrast to the spirit of his time. The seventeenth century believed in polemic religion; its weapons were argumentative heavy artillery and the cut and thrust of sharp dialectic, with no quarter asked or given. It grappled magnificently with great issues, it stooped to mean ones, with a partisan energy and thundering dogmatism hard to match in any period. It was an age of terrific invective whose readiest word for a distasteful argument was "heresy" or "atheism," and whose coarsest would no longer be printed. In a word, it was a day when Truth and Error were as real and as immutably opposed as God and the Devil. The controversies over bishop and king, Calvin and Arminius, Geneva and Canterbury, presbyter and priest fed the presses, both licensed and secret, with polemical folios, pamphlets, and sermons. The apologists went up and down the land, seeking whom they might devour. Taine compares them to mastadons, emerging from the primeval slime, and bristling with biblical and patristic proof-texts.

Browne is a different man, he belongs in another camp, and has another style. And since the texture of his language creates large parts of his meaning, it may be well to begin with the style.

It is a supremely great style, and like all styles of the highest class, in poetry or prose, it enters territories of meaning inaccessible to lesser talents. Some of these regions are its own solitary possession, but it is obviously a seventeenth-century style, and of a particular kind and following a particular fashion.

The manner was new then, in modern literature scarcely older than Montaigne. "It is an exercise to myself," Browne says in the preface. It is apparent that here is a writer, and a young one, who in the fashion of the time is thinking on paper, lighting his own darkness by flashes, trying honestly, yet with the artist's joy in the process, to show his thought in the making. There is none of the easy smoothness or elaborate rotundity of controversial writing. On the contrary there is imaginative brilliance, half-lights, the suggestive and stimulating sparkle of epigrams, truths half dug out like fragments of statues, frankness, discursiveness, point rather than clearness, delight in flashing the facets of a paradox, a subtle art that knows how to choose words that push into the inlets and winding shores of the mind.

Religio Medici is broadly an "informal essay," but that term is far too vague and too modern for our purposes. The style with which we are here concerned has been best described in a notable series of articles by Morris W. Croll.[1] In the last quarter of the sixteenth century there emerged in all the literary languages of Europe a new prose style, which developed hand in hand with the rise of rationalism and its new moral and scientific attitudes. It grew out of a revival of interest in the Stoic writers of the first Christian century, especially Seneca, and it caused both a revival of Stoicism and an imitation of the "Attic" style cultivated by the Stoics. Like its classical model it was an anti-Ciceronian movement. It rejected the oratorical, or "Asiatic," style, with its copiousness, rhetorical balance, floridity, and flowing ease. The movement was begun on the Continent by Muret, Lipsius, and Montaigne, and in England by Bacon. All of them had rejected the philosophical rigidity and complacence of the High Renaissance.

[1] Especially "Attic Prose in the Seventeenth Century," *Studies in Philology*, XVIII (April, 1921), 79–128; "Attic Prose: Lipsius, Montaigne, Bacon," *Schelling Anniversary Papers* (New York, 1923); "The Baroque Style in Prose," *Studies in English Philology: A Miscellany in Honor of Frederick Klaeber* (Minneapolis, 1929). The following remarks on style are almost entirely a digest of these articles.

In their independence, reserve, and scorn of easy knowledge and popular opinion they were virtually Stoics and they disdained the rotundities of accepted truths. The classical statement of their views in England is Bacon's famous attack in the *Advancement of Learning* on the vanities of learning. He condemns the "delicate learning" (the exclusive preoccupation with Ciceronian style), and the "magistral" method of exposition (which is dogmatic and aims only at persuasion), and he commends the aphoristic method, which he used not only in the *Essays* but the *Novum Organum*, because it presents the tentative and natural unfolding of ideas, not in their natural form, but as they actually grow in the mind.

This "Attic" or "Senecan" style or, as it was also called, "curt" style, aimed at expressiveness rather than formal beauty; it wished to convey the direct reality of individual experience in its full range. It imitated the simplicity and brevity of the Stoics, their curt wit and "point," their sententiousness, weight, and gravity, and that scorn of easy and vulgar knowledge which led to paradox and deliberate obscurity. It cultivated vigor, ease, and the flexible, subtle, intimate expressiveness of conversation. It had several strands, and in particular a further phase which Mr. Croll calls the "loose" style, as the most accurate description of its more expressive, freer, and more natural syntax. This developed with the growth of more searching and more skeptical philosophical attitudes. As the new rationalism came to its maturity the vogue of Stoicism declined and though the style was still Senecan, it found other models, particularly Rabelais. This is the style of the later Montaigne, and throughout the seventeenth century of the skeptical, "libertine" writers, and of all who to any degree were disposed to question the accepted verities.

But involved in the texture and tone of the Attic style are other qualities. It developed vices of its own. From too inordinate a striving for expressiveness and point it fell into a new kind of rhetorical extravagance and ornateness, as "Asiatic" or "Gothic" in its own way as the Ciceronianism that the Atticists wished to avoid, so that it can only be described as "a style of acute and condensed brevity, ornamented, at the same time, with the riches of rhetoric and an almost poetic splendor of words."[2]

---

[2] "Attic Prose: Lipsius, Montaigne, Bacon," p. 139.

Moreover, a part of this "splendor of words" derives from an innate and irresistible tendency of the Renaissance toward the pomp of empire, its grandeur and solemnity, and the rhetorical display that accompanied its ceremonial. Mr. Croll quotes a phrase of Bacon — "to persuade the King in greatness" — as an epitome of the literary obligation that fashioned the court tradition of occasional orations, especially funeral sermons, and the public reading of magniloquent poetry.

Finally, to all these characteristics must be added the all-pervading element of "imaginative conceit." In poetry the established word for this is "metaphysical," but this word has always been unsatisfactory and is scarcely available for prose. Yet some of the prose is highly "metaphysical." Confronted with all this complexity, Mr. Croll finally discards the term "Attic" and calls the style "baroque." Here, certainly, there are grounds for differing with him, for it will have to be admitted that this term is not altogether satisfactory. It is true that the word "baroque," though not yet really domesticated in English and American literary criticism, has long been applied on the Continent to literature as well as to the other arts as a critical label for certain aspects of this post-Renaissance style — its restless energy, intensity, sensuous colors, and the unity in diversity which it strove to reach through the ornate and clashing complexity of its designs. But the term "baroque," like much of the critical vocabulary, has been far too loosely defined and widely applied to be very serviceable.[3] The choice of a term here is of course difficult, but it seems doubtful whether "baroque" can cover all the stylistic traits of early seventeenth-century prose. Whether or not, however, we call the style "Attic," or "baroque," or something else, its characteristics are clear enough. It was a style partly inherited from the past, but "modified and indeed largely created by the profound moral experience which the age was undergoing. A prose-style that should adequately express this age must contrive, therefore, to mingle elements that in any other period would appear oddly contrasted. It must be at once ingenious and lofty, intense yet also profound, acute, realistic, revealing, but at the same time somewhat grave and mysterious. It must have in short that curious sublimity

[3] See René Wellek, "The Concept of Baroque in Literary Scholarship," *Journal of Aesthetics and Art Criticism*, V (1946), 77–109.

which is felt in the painting of El Greco, in the sermons and letters of Donne, and in certain sculptures of Bernini."[4]

Browne's style, as will be seen in the course of this study, has most of these traits. Its more strictly Attic elements — coolness, detachment, reserve, skeptical edge, distaste for bigotry and dogmatism — appear on the very first pages of *Religio Medici*. These are qualities that never arouse popular enthusiasm, and they certainly could not have done so in the 1630's. A generation which felt above all the crying need for action and which had leisure only to run a rough and martial finger down the pages might be excused for not knowing where to find Browne and this religion of his. Certainly from page to page there would appear to be the most marvelous chameleon changes of color — protective color, one hears the critics say. Consider from the contemporary point of view the drift of the most familiar outstanding passages. "For my religion," the book begins, "though there be several circumstances that might persuade the world I have none at all, as the general scandal of my profession, the natural course of my studies, the indifferency of my behavior and discourse in matters of religion, neither violently defending one, nor with that common ardor and contention opposing another; yet in despite hereof, I dare without usurpation assume the honorable style of a Christian."

This is a modest beginning, yet it might be thought definite enough. And he goes on to what seems like a clinching position: "There is no church whose every part so squares unto my conscience, whose articles, constitutions, and customs, seem so consonant unto reason, and, as it were, framed to my particular devotion, as this whereof I hold my belief, the church of England." In effect he declares himself to be a liberal Anglican, "neither believing this because Luther affirmed it, nor disapproving that because Calvin hath disavouched it," neither condemning Trent nor approving Dort wholesale. "In brief, where the Scripture is silent, the Church is my text; where that speaks, 'tis but my comment; where there is a joint silence of both, I borrow not the rules of my religion from Rome or Geneva, but the dictates of my own reason." Here is the familiar moderate platform of the Church of England.

[4] "Attic Prose: Lipsius, Montaigne, Bacon," p. 142.

But as we read on it soon becomes evident that Browne's Anglicanism is an astonishingly loose and mobile affair. "I could never divide myself from any man upon the difference of an opinion, or be angry with his judgment for not agreeing with me in that from which perhaps within a few days I should dissent myself." Not only is Browne obviously out of sympathy with the church militant; he shows a taint of the easy skepticism of Montaigne. Then comes another turn. "In philosophy, where truth seems double-faced, there is no man more paradoxical than myself; but in divinity I love to keep the road." The distinction was orthodox enough. Theology was abandoning her high prerogatives, and the separation of the natural and revealed had been the legitimate resort of science for some little time, but this proclamation of Browne has a distinctly provocative air. Instead of Bacon's grave and politic deference, there is a note of sly satisfaction. He goes on to say that while he hopes he has no taint of heresy, he must confess that his "greener studies have been polluted with two or three."

On the heels of this dubious position is a turn still more astonishing for its exuberance and irresponsibility. "As for those wingy mysteries in divinity, and airy subtleties in religion which have unhinged the brains of better heads, they never stretched the *pia mater* of mine. Methinks there be not impossibilities enough in religion for an active faith. . . . I love to lose myself in a mystery; to pursue my reason to an *O altitudo!*" Our physician is revealing himself as a full-fledged mystic, and we watch him in his first splendid flight. He is a new Tertullian, eager to explore the farthest reaches of that father's "odd resolution" — *certum est quia impossibile est*. He has already dropped that plodding figure of keeping the road. In this mood he throws out every ballast of reason and climbs into a rarefied and exhilarating atmosphere where it is intoxication to believe the most irrational things he can find in the Bible. It is a kind of spiritual gymnastics: "I desire to exercise my faith in the difficultest point." He will match his ability to believe with the most adept master of the age of faith — "and this I think is no vulgar part of faith, to believe a thing not only above but contrary to reason, and against the arguments of our proper senses." There are difficulties to be sure (and here is a leering gargoyle in the Gothic edifice), faith is not after all a cutting instrument. " 'Tis true, there is an edge in all firm belief, and with an easy metaphor we may say, the sword of faith; but in these obscurities I rather use it in the adjunct the apostle gives it, a buckler; under which I conceive a wary combatant may lie invulnerable." But what the century wanted was just this firm edge of belief and to cite the apostolic preference for a buckler rather than a sword was at the least an irritating reminder.

It would appear then that Browne thus early is committed to something very like mysticism. And the remainder of this passage deepens the impression. In the education of thirty years he has tamed his reason. He has reached the point where he is content to understand a mystery "in an easy and Platonic description." Beyond all the metaphysical definitions he loves the Hermetic description of God — *sphaera cuius centrum ubique, circumferentia nullibi*. He finds it good "to sit down with a description, periphrasis, or adumbration." Helpless before the mystery of the Trinity, he suddenly confesses that he has "often admired the mystical way of Pythagoras, and the secret magic of numbers." And hard upon this is a sentence in which he would seem finally to part company with the solid fabric of Christian cosmogony. "The severer schools shall never laugh me out of the philosophy of Hermes, that this visible world is but a picture of the invisible, wherein, as in a portrait, things are not truly, but in equivocal shapes, and as they counterfeit some more real substance in that invisible fabric."

But the reader has only begun to thread this labyrinth. The book is apparently a succession of moods which run the gamut of orthodox submission, persistent skepticism, mystical flights, scientific and philosophical argument, idle curiosity, and Stoic world-weariness — all imbedded in a discursive, intimately personal narrative. The book reveals strong enthusiasms and intellectual vigor, and very often a colorful love of life, but Browne is always interjecting remarks such as the following: "For the world, I count it not an inn, but an hospital; and a place not to live, but to die in. The world that I regard is myself; it is the microcosm of my own frame that I cast mine eye on; for the other, I use it but like my globe, and turn it round sometimes for my recreation."[5] He thanks God for his happy dreams only to add that "it is not a melancholy conceit to think we are all asleep in this world, and that the conceits of this life are as mere dreams to those of the next."[6] Toward the end he seems to confess himself finally a weary skeptic. In the round of philosophies we unlearn today what we learned tomorrow. "I have run through all sorts, yet find no rest in any . . . the wisest heads prove, at last, almost all Skeptics, and stand like Janus in the field of knowledge. I have therefore one common and authentic philosophy I learned in the schools, whereby I discourse and satisfy the reason of other men; another more reserved, and drawn from experience, whereby I content mine own."[7] Why not shut up our books? he says in another mood. A little longer and "we shall enjoy that by instinct and infusion, which we endeavor at here by labor and inquisition."[8]

One must read the book to catch the light from the facets of all these moods. To understand Browne requires sympathy and the kind of candor, humility, and untroubled powers of self-examination which he himself possessed. But these were not the salient characteristics of a morbidly troubled and militant generation. We are fascinated and charmed by his complexity, and wonder as a matter of secondary interest, whether he was more Catholic than Protestant, more skeptic than mystic. The readers of *Religio Medici* in the days of the Commonwealth asked these questions with real anxiety and acerbity. These things mattered immensely; in fact nothing else did matter. They found it difficult to label him, and he was edited admiringly by Puritan and Catholic editors respectively as a secret adherent of their faiths. But undoubtedly the commonest epithet, the readiest description then as always of unfamiliar thought, was "atheist." And a French librarian even circulated an amusing story that Browne, the declared enemy of all religion, having been expelled from Oxford for his debauches, retracted his beliefs late in life with proper penitence. It was a dangerous age for self-revelation on the subject of re-

[5] *Religio Medici*, II, 11.
[6] *Ibid.*
[7] II, 8.
[8] *Ibid.*

ligion. In the meantime in his circle of enlightened friends and among his Norwich neighbors and patients, Browne lived quietly all his life as an honored scientist and scholar and devout member of the Church of England.

Through the medium of these three hundred years it is certainly possible to see this extraordinary personality in a dispassionate light and to understand something of the complexities of his mind. They belong to an age that it is not easy for the modern mind to fathom. But baffling as the seventeenth century is in many of its aspects, it was fertile and creative almost beyond parallel, and, in order to estimate Browne's own qualities, it is important to relate him to its thought and its men of genius.

This must be done on broad lines, for the fine essence of Browne's thought lies under and between the lines, diffused everywhere, like the fluid soul of the old psychology, and no more to be distilled than the spirit of good poetry. The reader lives with it and finds it for himself. But we can at once distinguish two dominant traits. They lie on the surface and immediately impress any attentive reader. He has the attitude of romantic or transcendental faith, which is not seriously shaken by his skeptical inquiries; he has a pervading sympathy and charity. These two characteristics are controlling.

The quality of *Religio Medici* that first attracts our admiration is its unfailingly liberal spirit. From the author's first modest claim that he dare "without usurpation assume the honorable style of a Christian" to the fine passage near the close where he remarks that "no man can justly censure or condemn another; because indeed, no man truly knows another," this attitude, sane, winning, luminously pervading, is constantly maintained. Tolerance is a rare enough trait in any period, but in a time when the conflict of orthodoxies and the sharp resultant cleavages made skepticism a shocking disloyalty to the truth, it stands out in marked isolation.

II

The harsh sectarianism of Puritan England was in effect the inevitable first fruits of the Reformation, of the appeal which Protestantism had made from the authority of the Church to the conscience of every believer. This was the entering wedge of an individualism that eventually was to go far beyond the intentions of the Protestant Reformers, for they accepted the traditional theology and under the pressure of their political struggles the thing that they demanded was not intellectual freedom but authority. The result had been a Protestant Scholasticism more barren than any that preceded it, for instead of the authority of the Church they had set up a more dangerous standard — the rigid authority of the Bible, down to the last vowel points of the Hebrew manuscripts. This theology crystallized into a system as dogmatic as the Roman Catholic and more pessimistic. It retained the traditional thoroughgoing dualism that fixed a gulf between nature, subject to law, and revelation, subject to grace. The Reformers swept away the Catholic machinery of salvation, for they had their own doctrine of the way to bridge the gulf, but the gulf itself, so fundamental to historic Christianity was, if anything, widened and deepened. Milton's arduous attempt to moralize and beautify Protestant theology is a measure of its strength and weakness.

The attempt to rest on the infallibility of the Bible proved to be a desperate position, for it became evident at once that the Bible must be interpreted and that men do not agree on the interpretation. The Catholic Church possessed not only the inspired Bible but an inspired interpretation of it. The Protestants repudiated this interpretation, but not because of any tolerant or easy-going views about the meaning of the Bible or any wish to allow for differences of opinion. They believed that there could be but one meaning, not only in fundamentals but in all details, and that that meaning was the sacred Word of God. The inevitable result was that England, like all of Europe, was swarming with sects, each claiming to represent the divine mind and final truth. There were Anabaptists, Brownists, Familists, Socinians, Quakers, even a sect of divorcers who called themselves Miltonists! It was a phenomenon that violently irritated both Anglicans and Puritans. In a sense the Puritans were most outraged. Growingly dominant and imagining in this early flush of confidence that the Presbyterian church was the final chapter in the record of dispensations, the last word in orthodoxy, they cursed these sectarians in incredulous and impotent rage. In the language of one of their tracts, these sects were "the very dregs and spawn of old accursed heresies which had already been condemned, dead, buried, and rotten in their graves long ago." At its worst Protestantism was good meat become vermiculate, to use Bacon's harsh figure for the scholastic decay; at its best it showed the movement of the inquiring spirit which was its true genius. But the obvious situation was that every sectarian damned every other on the basis of his own interpretation of the Bible. In the struggle for a basis of ultimate authority the church as a whole, Puritan and Anglican, was the determined enemy of toleration.

It is easy to forget this. Puritanism held the stage, and its truly great services to English liberty tend to obscure the fact that these contributions were largely indirect and involuntary. As a movement it has thrown into the shade the truly liberal development of the English church, a development which found its adherents in moderate men of all camps and which, though it fought a losing battle at the time, began to show its effects after the Restoration. Moreover, the word "Puritan" came to be used so broadly by the end of the sixteenth century that it was little more than an emotional label. It was made to cover men of many sects and shades of opinion in and out of the Church of England. It would not be easy to determine at some points the difference between Sir Thomas Browne, the Anglican, and Colonel Hutchinson, the Puritan. There was a great deal of moderate opinion on each side, all through the revolutionary period; many were reluctant to take sides and finally did so with feelings of bitter despair.

Lord Falkland, remembered for his talents and charm and the death in action which he courted, was such a man. In the thirties, when Browne was writing *Religio Medici*, there habitually met at his house in Great Tew or in London that assemblage of scholars, statesmen, and poets celebrated in Suckling's "Sessions of the Poets." Among them were Chillingworth, Selden, Digby, Sandys, and Suckling himself. It is reported of Selden that he used to delight in confounding the learning and dogmatic opinionativeness of the Westminster divines. His *Table Talk* is full of blunt and sturdy opinions like the following: " 'Tis vain to talk of an heretic, for a man in his heart can think no otherwise than he does think." Suckling, who is more celebrated for sonnets to a pair of black eyes, once wrote a treatise entitled *An Account of Religion by Reason*. "Every man," he says in it, "that offers to give an account of religion by reason is suspected to have none at all," but it is hard to see "why a man should not use the best weapon his creator hath given him for his defense."

Liberalism drew strong inspiration from Holland, where the Arminians opposed Calvinism. Against rigid orthodoxy they asserted that the infallibility of Scripture was not an external power to be wielded by the Church but belonged to the private judgment. They also made the fruitful distinction between fundamental and non-fundamental doctrines. John Hales was one of the Englishmen who went to the Synod of Dort in 1619 to defend predestination against Arminian free will. Dort saw the defeat of the Arminians and the counter-formulation of the famous five points of Calvinism, but none the less Calvinism in its harsher forms was on the wane in England and the High-Church party espoused Arminianism. At Dort Hales underwent a celebrated conversion, though not altogether to Arminianism, and, as he said, "bade good night to John Calvin." There was a large body of sane and moderate men like these, equally opposed to Laud and Pym, and finally overborne only by the intolerance and tragic blunders of both sides.

Religio Medici can be better understood if we indicate briefly the direction of liberal religious philosophy up to the mid-century. The opposition of Canterbury and Geneva had begun early in the reign of Elizabeth. Moderate statesmen and theologians had understood the danger involved in the issues and had endeavored by every means to postpone and if possible avert fatal conflict. By far the greatest of these was Richard Hooker. The *Ecclesiastical Polity*, which he brought out in the 1590's in defense of Anglicanism against the Puritans, transcends by its sweep and depth of thought and irenic temper all partisan controversy, and becomes the loftiest statement of rational religion in the history of English thought. Its intellectual grasp and spiritual power are almost ideal. Hooker laid down for many a succeeding century the true foundation of religion — "the eternal law laid up in the bosom of God," not an arbitrary law but that law which is in the nature of God himself, "which he himself hath perpetually purposed to keep," the broad rationalizing principle of the universe. All spheres of life, natural and revealed, are aspects of the one law of reason. In the realm of faith the will is dependent on reason, for man is a lover of the good and naturally chooses it, and reason must be in every act of faith. The Bible is inspired, but to it belongs not the ordering of indifferent matters, but the grand spheres of action which often lead men out beyond its commands, and its authority is tested by reason. As for the tests of reason the general judgment of society must be respected, for few individuals have reasoning powers sufficient for sustained and deep investigation: "The general and perpetual voice of men is as the sentence of God himself." Yet this is not infallible, for commonly held opinions are often errors and need to be overthrown. In social organization the particular form of government is a matter of expediency and the consent of the governed is necessary.

Hooker had a conservative regard for the Catholic tradition, and in defending the reasonableness of historic Christianity he followed the broad arguments of Thomas Aquinas. But he went behind orthodoxies, both Catholic and Protestant, to something deeper, and here he defined the real meaning of English Protestantism and gave it personality and a new sense of direction. The Bible must not be made the platform of a new and narrower orthodoxy. It is not the whole of human knowledge; it presupposes moral truths, known to man before it was written, and the capacity to understand them, and its validity can be tested only in the light of reason. And Hooker added to all these intellectual faculties a singular gentleness of spirit. "There will come a time," he says, "when three words uttered with charity and meekness shall receive a far more blessed reward than three thousand volumes written with disdainful sharpness of wit."

In the generation immediately following, as the revolution loomed up, the concern was to hold the nation together, and the emphasis had to change. The question of religious authority could no longer be argued with Hooker's serenity and breadth but was narrowed sharply and decisively to meet the rival claims of High Church and Puritan to divine right. Bacon may be taken as representative of the statesman who has no vital interest in religious controversies but deplores their political and social effects. Like Hooker he points out the difference between fundamentals and non-fundamentals, and argues against insisting on complete perfection in doctrine. He thinks unity possible, but not on the basis either of enforced conformity or patched-up compromises. In his essays "Of Unity in Religion" and "Of Superstition," both published in 1612, he shows that contempt for the popular judgment which was so strong a feature of the times — ironic in Hooker, derisive and sometimes savage in Burton, and the most positive trait in the quiet Browne, the cause possibly of his Stoic abstention from public affairs. Bacon uses strong language on this topic: "The master of superstition is the people; and in all superstition wise men follow fools." He feels that "as the temporal sword is to be drawn with great circumspection in cases of religion, so is it a monstrous thing to put it into the hands of the common people." To make war in the name of religion is to fly on the ship of the church "a flag of a bark of pirates and assassins. Therefore," he says with great energy, "it is most necessary that the church . . . do damn and send to hell forever those facts and opinions tending to the support of the same."

In the decade when Browne was producing *Religio Medici* in the solitude of Shipden Hall, the outstanding defenders of toleration and the reasonableness of religion were Hales, Falkland, and Chillingworth. Hales' *Tract Concerning Schism and Schismatics* and Falkland's *Discourse of the Infallibility of the Church of Rome* were written in the thirties and published a few years later. Chillingworth's *The Religion of Protestants a Safe Way to Salvation* (1637) was written in part at Great Tew. Hales clearly lays down the principle that salvation depends on nothing but sincere love toward God and Christ. Bare errors of the understanding cannot damn anyone. "The things necessary to be known unto salvation are few and very simple and easy to be understood by the simplest." "They are heretics who are condemned of their own conscience." Falkland argues to the same effect. "To those who follow their reason in the interpretation of the Scripture God will either give his grace for assistance to find the truth or his pardon if they miss it. And then this supposed necessity of an infallible guide (with the supposed damnation for the want of it) fall together to the ground."

Chillingworth's book was more influential and drew more fire.

It was a defense of the biblical religion of Protestants against the Roman Church, written after his conversion to Rome and return to Protestantism, and hence deals only indirectly with the questions at issue between Anglicans and Puritans. It defends on broad lines the authority of the Bible. But the Bible, if Protestantism is true to itself, cannot be narrowly and irrationally interpreted. The Bible is clear to every honest mind in its essentials, he says; nothing need be believed but what is plainly revealed. Every man can only use his best endeavor. For the orthodox, Chillingworth was an unwelcome defender of Protestantism, and his latitudinarianism linked him, as Milton's also did, with the free-thinking Socinians.

In the forties the greatest pleas for liberty and toleration were the Puritan *Areopagitica* (1644) and the High-Church *Liberty of Prophesying* (1647). The former is the only one of the books here mentioned that is now generally read, but it was little noticed in 1644, and of far less effect than Roger Williams' *Bloody Tenent of Persecution*, published in the same year. *Areopagitica* is an early evidence of Milton's gradual disillusionment. He is proceeding leftward from the Presbyterians to the Independents, who of all the contemporary sects might be called the best nursery of toleration. Finally, also on the Puritan side, were the Cambridge Platonists, who began to teach and write in the fifties. More must be said of them later on, but to enlarge further here on Milton and Taylor and the Cambridge Platonists would be to erect a very heavy church porch for the delicate structure of *Religio Medici*. The massive columns and broad steps of the *Ecclesiastical Polity* or *Areopagitica* must not be allowed to cover up the chapel behind.

III

Religio Medici belongs to the class of informal books whose intention is candid self-revelation rather than argument. It is discursive, leisurely, often gossipy, and its ideas have to be washed out like fragments of ore from the loose mass. But on the other hand it is so conscious and elaborate a work of art and it has such frequent passages of sinewy exposition, fairly scholastic in their gravity, that any loose classification fails to describe it. Perhaps no classification is possible; the book is *sui generis*. But one thing is clear: there is no definite controversial issue, no sharp intellectual outline. There might be a hint of challenge in the title, an implication that a physician and layman is invading the theologian's field, as having a right to think for himself, and something to say. Indeed, according to Keck, the earliest annotator, this was not overlooked. He notes that "exception by some hath been taken to it in respect of its inscription, as though physicians had a religion by themselves," and he hastens to explain that the author merely wants to defend physicians against their vulgar reputation as atheists. No doubt the title is not a challenge, but simply an announcement that here in all humility is a tentative statement of personal religious conviction. "It is an exercise to myself," says Browne in the preface. We have, then, as in Montaigne, philosophy assuming the "liberty of conversation."

But there is a striking difference from the outset. Instead of Montaigne's debonair, bluff honesty, we have the utmost gravity and reserve and caution. In fact the preface seems almost painfully timid. It is true that the two pirated editions of 1642 had been full of gross corruptions and misprints, and Browne was justified in complaining of this "depraved copy," but apart from correcting these blunders the authorized edition has no really important differences.[9] Browne's hesitation, therefore, to release and acknowledge his book looks almost like a case of nerves. He insists that he has penned "rather a memorial unto me, than an example or rule unto any other," explains possible lapses on the ground of being compelled to write away from his library, protests that the opinions of "many years past" are not necessarily his present ones, begs the reader to consider that "there are many things delivered rhetorically, many expressions therein merely tropical, to be taken in a soft and flexible sense, and not to be called unto the rigid test of reason," and finally declares that as for his opinions he will "no further father them than the best and most learned judgments shall authorize them." Surely, to use his own phrase, under the buckler of such a preface this wary Dr. Browne should be able to "lie invulnerable." All this is in

[9] Olivier Leroy, in his *Le Chevalier Thomas Browne* (Paris, 1931) pp. 379 ff., has shown this conclusively. He rightly points out that most critics of Browne, including the present writer, have minimized the corruptions of the 1642 editions, and many have drawn the false conclusion that Browne markedly toned down his ideas in the authorized edition.

the strongest possible contrast to the forthright vigor of the controversialists just mentioned.

But *Religio Medici* is neither timid nor shifty nor easily indifferent. If various contemporary readers could not decide whether the author was a Puritan or a Catholic or an atheist, it was not so much because he was slyly and prudently evasive as because they could not understand him. It is to be considered, too, whether modern critics of Browne like Hazlitt and Gosse do not also misunderstand him. Hazlitt, contrasting him with Montaigne, says that he has no moral character because he loves a paradox more than the truth. But Browne's ability to hold both sides of a paradox at once does not make him contemptible. Hazlitt might have remembered a remark of Montaigne himself: "We are, I know not how, of a double nature, so that what we believe we do not believe." There was plenty of the subtle Brahma in the author of the *Essais*. In something of a milder spirit Gosse concludes that Browne's career was a lifelong compromise, and he contrasts what he calls his "easy optimism," his prosperous occupation of collecting birds' eggs and attending church in Norwich, with Pascal's agonized repudiation of the science of his youth.[10] Browne, he says, was never troubled with the ascetic scruples of Pascal. This is no doubt true. But the fact that Browne's religious doubts did not compel him to abandon science with Pascal does not prove him Jesuitical or trifling.

The fact is that in this fierce concentration of the age on the opposition of faith and reason, Sir Thomas Browne takes a position which, while it lacks anything like intellectual sharpness, is yet clear and steady in its general principles. For all his irenic spirit, he speaks out vigorously enough on matters that are fundamental for him. He was above everything a Christian, and a Christian whose religion was more spirit than dogma. Dowden has characterized him perfectly in a phrase borrowed from Donne: "All divinity is love or wonder." There could be no better epitome of Browne or of the metaphysical poets, whom he so much resembles. This is the temper which controls Browne's rationalism. He is a sincere member of the Church of England, unquestionably honest in his submission to her authority, because he finds there, or so believes, the most inclusive philosophy.

[10] *Op. cit.*, pp. 65 ff.

To such a man the chief value of the creeds and the institution is that they furnish a symbol for the indefinable objects of faith. To him the hospitable Protestantism of the English church, which is the heir of the Gothic, many columned, shadowy Scholasticism of the Middle Ages, has room for "Lord Christ's heart and Plato's brain," for Aristotle and Plotinus and many another. He is a true Protestant in that the Bible is worth more than all these, but the Bible itself is no white light; it, too, in Browne's best loved figure, is but the shadow of God.

In other words Browne is a religious romanticist. His thought lacks the sharp outlines of Calvin's or Bacon's or Hooker's. Like all these he draws a separating line between the natural and the revealed, but he does it in a different way. Calvin draws the line in order to separate lost man from sovereign God; Bacon draws it in order to mark off a workable field of knowledge; Hooker draws it to safeguard both the uniqueness of the Bible and the validity of the Christian experience. Browne is closest to Hooker, and he needed the vast theological edifice of the Middle Ages, like a cathedral of many periods and styles, where Aristotle and Augustine meet; but whereas Hooker had derived from Scholasticism a coherent and rational philosophy, Browne loves to roam in other regions of it — the mystical. The noteworthy thing is that he draws less from Thomas Aquinas than from Tertullian.

"I love to lose myself in a mystery; to pursue my reason to an *O altitudo.*" That is probably the key to the whole. One returns to the passage which is built up around this sentence[11] with a deepening conviction that it explains everything in Browne. Here he first uses those two symbols which seem to have captured his imagination more than any other: the mystical circle of God whose center is everywhere and whose circumference nowhere,[12] and the divine adumbration — *Lux est umbra Dei.* He uses both again and again. "There is no such thing as solitude," he says later in *Religio Medici,* "nor anything that can be said to be alone, and by itself, but God, who is his own circle, and can subsist by himself."[13] The devils cannot fly from God, he says once in *Vulgar Errors,* "until they can get out of Trismegistus his

---

[11] *Religio Medici,* I, 9 and 10.
[12] Attributed in a note by Browne to Hermes Trismegistus. Greenhill says it cannot be found in the writings that go under that name.
[13] *Religio Medici,* II, 10.

circle, that is, to extend their wings above the universe, and pitch beyond ubiquity." [14] He touches on it again in *The Garden of Cyrus*, where he reminds us that the mystical name of God "emphatically sets forth the notion of Trismegistus, and that intelligible sphere, which is the nature of God." [15] And finally in *Christian Morals*: "Trismegistus his circle, whose center is everywhere, and circumference nowhere, was no hyperbole. Words cannot exceed, where they cannot express enough. Even the most winged thoughts fall at the setting out, and reach not the portal of divinity." [16] The other symbol—light is the shadow of God—determines the imagery of *Urn Burial*, and is worked up through a long and glowing passage in Chapter IV into the really final cadence of *The Garden of Cyrus*.

So where Hooker speaks of the eternal reason, "laid up in the bosom of God," or Calvin of the divine decree, Browne takes refuge in two unthinkable paradoxes. In these obscurities, he tells us in this early passage in *Religio Medici*, it is good to sit down with "an adumbration; for by acquainting our reason how unable it is to display the visible and obvious effects of nature, it becomes more humble and submissive unto the subtleties of faith; and thus I teach my haggard and unreclaimed reason to stoop unto the lure of faith." This falcon metaphor is a beautiful and, it seems, a daringly inverted one, with its notion of soaring reason flying at the sun to be enticed to earth by the lure of faith. But we see Browne's bent. Bacon, setting the method of scientific investigation for the future, points out how clumsy were the Schoolmen's logical tools beside the infinite subtleties of nature and taught his generation to track her by keeping the eye on the object and trusting to the mind and senses in combination. But Browne is first poet and then scientist. And in the realm of imagination, which was his peculiar domain, reason and sense alike were "haggard" and unreclaimed.

As he goes on in this mood he is not to be stayed by strange Bible absurdities which he mentions, such as the Mosaic botany which had a tree in Eden before plants were created. He rushes to embrace them, as he will many others (though he is never

[14] *Vulgar Errors*, I, ii.
[15] *The Garden of Cyrus*, chap. v.
[16] *Christian Morals*, III, 2.

able to refrain from citing them at length), and proceeds to the first exercise of his faith "in the difficultest point" — to contemplate eternity. It is the first flight of haggard reason, and we see what an imagination like Browne's can do with the idea of predestination. "Time we may comprehend; 'tis but five days elder than ourselves," but who can speak of God's infinity? Yet Browne's powers kindle at the notion. "In eternity there is no distinction of tenses; and therefore that terrible term predestination, which hath troubled so many weak heads to conceive, and the wisest to explain, is in respect to God no prescious determination of our estate to come, but a definitive blast of his will already fulfilled, and at the instant that he first decreed it; for to his eternity, which is indivisible and all together, the last trump is already sounded, the reprobates in the flame, and the blessed in Abraham's bosom." Here is William James' "block universe, eternal and without a history," completely set forth in one stroke with the swift vision of a mystic. "What to us is to come," it goes on, "to his eternity is present, his whole duration being but one permanent point, without succession, parts, flux, or division." If we want to conceive the dizzying paradox of supralapsarianism, Browne will push that tremendous Calvinist principle to its farthest for us.

So with the mystery of the Trinity. It is a fearful domain, but enchanted for Browne. He loves to call to his aid "the mystical way of Pythagoras, and the secret magic of numbers" to help him think of the number three as not divided but comprehended in its unity. "Beware of philosophy," yes, but nature carries on her forehead the "stenography and short characters" of divinity, and he is haunted by the persistent conviction that "this visible world is but a picture of the invisible," a portrait merely, a counterfeit of real substance in the invisible fabric.

Then follows a final preliminary flight, on the subject of another attribute of God — his wisdom. "We behold him but asquint, upon reflex or shadow" and to pry into his counsels is folly in man and presumption in angels, but, nevertheless, Browne cannot resist a metaphysical disquisition on the union of thought and act in the Trinity, before retreating to the safe ground of natural philosophy.

It is clear enough, then, that Browne was chiefly attracted to the imaginative side of religion, that its formal definitions never hedged him in but were felt to be a limitless champaign for him to stray in, and that with a mystical catholicism he borrowed his ideas as often from Trismegistus or the Cabbala as from the Bible. His famous boast that he believed in impossibilities is of course outstanding. Alongside of Hooker or Thomas Aquinas or the hard theology of the Puritans it seems naive. But it would be rash on the basis of this to call Browne hopelessly irrational. For one thing it is well to remember that the passage in question does not throw reason to the winds. After all it simply takes the familiar position that the articles of faith will always be found rational when tested by the slower and more feeble faculties of reason. When he says that there are not impossibilities enough in religion he means that the dogmas are too easily understandable to offer imagination any scope: "The deepest mysteries ours contains have not only been illustrated, but maintained, by syllogism and the rule of reason." Then again, the epigram like much in Browne is a buoyant exaggeration. We shall see that in many a case his own reason is his "best Oedipus." The point of view is really only the familiar attitude of faith. As Bishop Westcott said, *Credo ut intellegam* and *Intellego ut credam* are both true at different levels. Browne's catholic willingness to believe means primarily in his case a very positive acceptance of the realm of religious imagination. He is above all undogmatic. He is not indifferent, nor simply a speculative dreamer; he believes intensely that the world has a purpose and man a destiny, and he accepts the Christian teaching about both, but he sees it as "love and wonder" transcending the creeds.

IV

The other determining element in his temperament is his unfailing spirit of charity. Browne divided *Religio Medici* into two parts, evidently intending to introduce a certain element of order, as though faith had been the subject of the first part, and it now became him to speak of charity. But the whole is so rambling and its ideas are so interwoven that the division strikes one as an afterthought. At any rate the spirit of charity upon which he begins to expatiate in the second book so pervades and determines the whole that by a kind of higher logic it ought to come first. As he says in the beginning of this part, it is a virtue "without which faith is a mere notion and of no existence." In the charming gossip of these later pages he describes his freedom from every kind of prejudice. "I have no antipathy, or rather idiosyncrasy, in diet, humor, air, anything." He has none of the antipathies that he discovers in others, no national repugnances. "I was born in the eighth climate, but seem for to be framed and constellated unto all. I am no plant that will not flourish out of a garden. All places, all airs, make unto me one country; I am in England everywhere, and under any meridian." In short he protests on his conscience that he hates no essence unconditionally but the devil. It is simply a reaffirmation of that spirit, rare for a seventeenth-century Englishman, which in the early pages of the first part inspires his quick sympathy for religious customs and beliefs different from his own. Browne was a natural cosmopolitan and his foreign travels had broadened instead of narrowing his sympathies. He saw the beauty of Catholic ceremonies in France and Italy.[17] "At the sight of a cross, or crucifix, I can dispense with my hat, but scarce with the thought or memory of my Savior," he says, remembering those days. "I could never hear the Ave Mary bell without an elevation, or think it a sufficient warrant, because they erred in one circumstance, for me to err in all, that is, in silence and dumb contempt." And when his comrades and fellow students have "fallen into an excess of scorn and laughter" at sight of a religious procession on the street, he confesses that he has "wept abundantly." He is conscious of such a warmth of natural charity that he feels obliged to apologize for it as a kind of selfishness, as "moral charity," and hastens to explain that he gives alms not for virtue's sake but to fulfill God's commands.[18] He is struck by the ability of beggars to single out a friendly face, and he muses on the wonders of physiognomy — that "there are mystically in our faces certain characters which carry in them the motto of our souls, wherein he that cannot read A B C may read our natures." He cannot relieve a beggar with his purse without asking a prayer for his soul, for, he says in a beautiful passage, "there is under these centoes and miserable outsides, those mutilate and semi-bodies, a soul of the same alloy

[17] *Religio Medici*, I, 2.
[18] II, 2.

with our own, whose genealogy is God as well as ours, and in as fair a way to salvation as ourselves." [19] This has the simple and unaffected brotherliness of a St. Francis.

Browne's charity is partly mystical. Behind it, he confesses himself, is the conviction that "all that is truly amiable is God, or as it were a divided piece of him, that retains a reflex or shadow of himself." [20] But it is more. It grows, too, out of a delicately sympathetic understanding of human frailty and limitation. In this respect he is a prototype of Charles Lamb. He uses the very words so often associated with Lamb: "No man can justly censure or condemn another; because, indeed, no man truly knows another." [21] Lamb may have found them here. He finds it true for himself, Browne goes on, that even for his nearest friends he is in a cloud, and only God sees him truly. Not only so, but "no man can judge another, because no man knows himself." "I find there are many pieces in this one fabric of man; this frame is raised upon a mass of antipathies." [22] He finds himself to be a "world of contrarieties": "Let me be nothing, if within the compass of myself I do not find the battle of Lepanto, passion against reason, reason against faith, faith against the devil, and my conscience against all." [23] How can any man, that is, who has ever looked into himself judge another?

It is at these two points of love and wonder, the imaginative aspect of religion and the spirit of charity, that Browne's liberalism expresses itself. And it does so with no little vigor. The two traits are inextricably mingled, but as we go through *Religio Medici* we see that it is the violation of one or the other that provokes his protests. He is a Christian, he had said in the very beginning, in those beautifully tempered and measured words whose spirit and cadence remind one of Hooker: "To be particular, I am of that reformed new-cast religion, wherein I dislike nothing but the name; of the same belief our Savior taught, the Apostles disseminated, the fathers authorized, and the martyrs confirmed; but by the sinister ends of princes, the ambition and avarice of prelates, and the fatal corruption of times so decayed, impaired,

[19] II, 13.
[20] II, 14.
[21] II, 4.
[22] II, 7.
[23] *Ibid.*

and fallen from its native beauty, that it required the careful and charitable hands of these times to restore it to its primitive integrity." Yet as a reformer he has not "shaken hands" with the Catholic Church: "We have reformed from them, not against them"; there is a common Christian faith and body of principles. And, he continues, with the level judgment of a historian, there have been many reformers and many reformations, each country proceeding according to its national interest or temperament or climate. But though he dislikes the name Protestant, he finds that the Church of England as a whole squares best with his conscience and reason; he subscribes to her articles in essentials; the order of authority is roughly Bible, church, and reason. This is his platform.

It is after this liberal and sympathetic statement that he is roused to his first protest. It is on the subject of those scurrilities of language which served divines and laymen on both sides instead of arguments. These were the accustomed religious civilities of the day. But Browne has no patience with those zealous co-religionists of his who for "heretic" flung back in the teeth of the Catholics "antichrist," "man of sin," or the popular and more picturesque "whore of Babylon." He acknowledges the "duty of good language." "It is the method of charity to suffer without reaction," he remarks gravely, and though this rhetoric of the pulpiteer may delight the vulgar, it in no wise confirms the faith of wise believers, "who know that a good cause needs not be patroned by passion." The tone reminds us of a reply that Hooker once made to his adversary: "Your next argument consists of railing and of reasons: to your railing, I say nothing; to your reasons, I say what follows."

It is this habit of insensate railing instead of cool and sympathetic consideration that provokes a superb protest against dogmatism. Browne here first reveals his epigrammatic quality. The thrusts are deadly and not to be parried, and delivered with the coolest courtesy. "I could never divide myself from any man upon the difference of an opinion, or be angry with his judgment for not agreeing with me in that from which, perhaps within a few days I should dissent myself." [24] What roars of rage would this evoke from those bigots who were defending "the faith once

[24] I, 6.

delivered to the saints"! "I have no genius to disputes in religion; and have often thought it wisdom to decline them, especially upon a disadvantage, or when the cause of truth might suffer in the weakness of my patronage." Such a stroke severs the weak head from many a gesticulating body, but it leaves the owner standing and disputing. The coarser invectives of Burton or Butler were more obvious. The rest must be quoted: "Where we desire to be informed, 'tis good to contest with men above ourselves; but to confirm and establish our opinions, 'tis best to argue with judgments below our own, that the frequent spoils and victories over their reasons may settle in ourselves an esteem and confirmed opinion of our own. Every man is not a proper champion for truth, nor fit to take up the gauntlet in the cause of verity. Many, from the ignorance of these maxims, and an inconsiderate zeal unto truth, have too rashly charged the troops of error and remain as trophies unto the enemies of truth. A man may be in as just possession of truth as of a city, and yet be forced to surrender; 'tis therefore far better to enjoy her with peace than to hazard her on a battle."

This is not only consummate phrase making; it has the resolute vigor of a thoughtful man who knew his age through and through, and though no doubt it shows personal humility, it has the thrust of a shrewd attack, which Browne takes no pains to conceal, and which is the more telling, in the end at least, for its evident modesty. Not many years after, Benjamin Whichcote, the first Cambridge Platonist, wrote, "How much easier is it quietly to enjoy, than eagerly to contest! How vastly wiser!" The two men think alike. Both had loyalty to truth, and both were capable, at the proper challenge, of fighting for it, but both knew the difference between blind partisan strife and that search for truth which, as Bacon says, is "the love making or wooing of it." So in the year 1635 or thereabouts Sir Thomas Browne serenely refuses to take part in the strife of tongues.

His way is to forget or defer his doubts and to wait for better light, for, as he puts it in a characteristic epigram, "I perceive every man's reason is his best Oedipus." And then follows the famous remark: "In philosophy, where truth seems double-faced, there is no man more paradoxical than myself; but in divinity I love to keep the road." This again looks like timidity, this eagerness to "follow the great wheel of the church" in humble faith, keeping his mind swinging in the safe orbit of orthodoxy, and the passage is usually cited to point that view of Browne.[25] But perhaps the profession that he loves to "keep the road" is intended partly as a rebuke to presumptuous sectarians. For as he goes on to talk about heresy in his quiet way there is no impression of timidity.

His easy, indifferent tone is eminently calculated to enrage the orthodox. As for heresies, he confides to us in a quaintly humorous way, he must confess that his "greener studies have been polluted with two or three" — not new heresies, to be sure, but old and obsolete, appropriate to an antiquarian head like his. The fact, he ventures blandly to think, is an illustration of the eternally recurrent cycle of opinions. This easy levity would scarcely please that divine who characterized contemporary sects as "the very dregs and spawn of old accursed heresies which had been already condemned, dead, buried, and rotten in their graves long ago."

These cherished heresies of his were three in number and at his confession of each one it is not easy to resist the conviction that he is delivering a quiet thrust at some weak joint in the armor of the sectarians. "Now the first of mine was that of the Arabians; that the souls of men perished with their bodies, but should yet be raised again at the last day."[26] His apology for this venerable belief, which Milton too held,[27] is worth noticing: "Surely it is but the merits of our unworthy natures, if we sleep in darkness until the last alarum. A serious reflex upon my own unworthiness did make me backward from challenging this prerogative of my soul: so that I might enjoy my Savior at the last,

---

[25] The next sentence reads, "By this means I leave no gap for heresy, schisms, or errors, of which at present, I hope I shall not injure truth to say I have no taint or tincture." The pirated editions of 1642 had printed, "I shall injure truth to say," etc. W. A. Greenhill, followed by others, thought that the earlier version, supported by three MS copies, represented an admission of heresies which Browne withdrew in 1643. But the 1642 version makes such confused sense in its context that it looks like a simple misprint. Leroy (*op. cit.*, p. 383), though he is right, I think, in regarding this sentence as either a copyist's or a printer's corruption, confuses the case by his mistaken reading — "I hope I shall injure truth" etc.

[26] I, 7.

[27] For a discussion of Milton's belief in mortalism see Denis Saurat, *Milton: Man and Thinker* (London, 1944 ed.), pp. 119 ff. and 268.

FAITH AND REASON

I could with patience be nothing almost unto eternity." That "almost unto eternity" is one of Browne's subtlest turns. Is he not rebuking here the haughty presumption that salvation is a prerogative? And the impression deepens when we come to the second heresy. He had believed, with many Church Fathers, in universalism — "that God would not persist in his vengeance for ever," "which error," he says, "I fell into upon a serious contemplation of the great attribute of God, his mercy; and did a little cherish it myself, because I found therein no malice, and a ready weight to sway me from the other extreme of despair, whereunto melancholy and contemplative natures are too easily disposed." Now this is not only a shrewd analysis of morbid Puritan psychology; it is a quiet examination of the morals of the Puritan God, for to a man of humanitarian instincts "malice" was the only word that could account for Him. His third mild heresy — one which, by the way, has at length been adopted by the Church of England — had been a sympathy for the rite of prayers for the dead, a custom which Browne says he had almost instinctively been drawn to. It is clear that he regards these early aberrations of his not only with tolerance, but perhaps with a lingering affection. He even feels that they show aspects of truth which like the ghost of Banquo will not down in spite of official repudiation.

It must be admitted, however, that Sir Thomas is very evasive here. As we read on, we are bound to confess that he takes a too obvious delight in contemplating the play of "singular opinions and conceits of all ages," in the revolutions of heresies and super-heresies "wherein the liberty of an honest reason may play and expatiate with security, far without the circle of an heresy." Then come thick and fast his debonair and offhand treatment of "wingy mysteries," the "riddle" of the Trinity, the *certum est quia impossibile est*, the buckler of faith for the wary believer, and finally some really acute biblical criticism. The charge of atheism is, all in all, at least understandable.

Furthermore, his theory of heresy is far from militant. To be heresies, he says, opinions must be imparted to others and propagated, and since he had not done this, his were not heresies, but "bare errors" in which his will had no part. Of course this is weak logic. It implies for one thing that the given opinion is wrong. In effect Sir Thomas begs the question: the *wrong* opinion kept to myself is not heresy. Compared with men like Hales or Taylor, Browne at this point is certainly feeble. The villainy of Lucifer, he says curiously enough, was that he "was not content to err alone, but drew into his faction many legions of spirits." Milton's dramatic portrait of that mighty personage as a kind of supernatural Cromwell measures the difference between a man like Browne and the great controversialists.

But if he came short of heroism or even of clear-headedness, he had what seemed to him and to most moderate men in 1635 a sufficient warrant for his position. The watchword of "the Truth" from either prelate or Presbyterian did not seem to him to challenge much enthusiasm. He could not escape the conviction that neither party had a monopoly of that commodity, and he realized clearly that the inevitable end of sectarianism was hopeless bigotry. In the existing situation that was the cardinal sin. It was the disease of the time. How crushing is his remark that "those have not only depraved understandings, but diseased affections, which cannot enjoy a singularity without a heresy, or be the author of an opinion without they be of a sect also."[28] That "enjoy a singularity" carries a barbed contempt. It is simply the position of moderate churchmen throughout the war: that for the sake of national unity the Thirty-nine Articles were to be regarded not as essentials of faith but as "instruments of peace." This of course raises the whole question of religious liberty. In the thirties the Puritan-Anglican controversy probably went too far and the issues became too sharp for compromise to be possible. When Archbishop Ussher said authoritatively of the Thirty-nine Articles that the Church does not "oblige any man to believe them, but only not to contradict them," he is intending to offer a basis for latitudinarian compromise, but he is not proposing toleration of dissent. Political toleration was not yet thought possible; it had to develop indirectly and involuntarily from the refusal of sects to be exterminated, and the cost of it was civil war. Browne does not face this issue. His position, like Hooker's and the Cambridge Platonists', is spiritual rather than political. "How much easier is it quietly to enjoy than eagerly to contest! How vastly wiser!" Whichcote writes. In the same

[28] I, 7.

way Browne says, in rebuking the folly of useless martyrdom, "The leaven, therefore, and ferment of all not only civil, but religious actions is wisdom." [29] He hates dogmatism because it obscures the truth and disturbs the peace which are the heart of religion. The schismatic glares at a narrow point until it becomes his whole field of vision; the man of loftier mind knows that the way to extend truth is by sympathy, for truth is partial and can be extended.

V

In connection with these self-confessed heresies of Browne, something may be said about his biblical criticism. He is celebrated for a persistent tendency to notice inconsistencies and improbabilities in the Bible. He himself says he has been tempted by the devil to find naturalistic explanations for biblical miracles, and he makes a point of his struggles with doubt: "There is as in philosophy, so in divinity, sturdy doubts, and boisterous objections, wherewith the unhappiness of our knowledge too nearly acquainteth us. More of these no man hath known than myself, which I confess I conquered, not in a martial posture, but on my knees." [30] It is hard to believe that these struggles were severe, but he raises many questions about biblical events, some grotesque and quaint, others more weighty, and *Vulgar Errors* reopens them in one form or another. How did the pigeon sent out from the ark find her mate? Where was Lazarus' soul during his interment? Who will have Adam's lost rib at the resurrection? In what season was the world created? More seriously, Why may not the water which Elijah used for his miracle have been naphtha? How on the basis of the Noah's ark story shall we account for the distribution of animal life in all continents? This, says Browne almost maliciously, "put the honest father to the refuge of a miracle." [31] How explain the contradictory accounts of the death of Judas and the tower of Babel? His pages are enlivened with a great deal more of this sort of thing, and his answers to these questions and to many others like them create much of

[29] *Religio Medici*, I, 26.
[30] *Ibid.*, I, 26.
[31] Sir Thomas refrains from advancing the highly amusing theory of those days that travelers, for some unfathomable reason, transported wild beasts to foreign shores in their ships.

that flavor of mixed credulity and skepticism for which he is so famous.

But such a compartmental attitude toward the Bible is common enough even today. And before the real advent of the higher criticism it was altogether natural. In a little while both the Bible itself and miracles were to become liabilities rather than assets; but in Browne's day this stage had not been reached. Science had not yet demonstrated the fallibility of the Bible, or established the principle of invariable law so firmly as to be embarrassed by biblical miracles. Browne could still say of his doubts, as he does quaintly, that "the devil played at chess with me, and yielding a pawn, thought to gain a queen of me." He sees difficulties, but the traditional faith seems invulnerable and he dismisses them as unimportant. He lived in a world which was saturated with miracle, and for him peculiarly so. "There is not one miracle greater than another," he insists. And he feels this so strongly that he hesitates to take the usual Protestant position — that miracles ceased with the apostolic age. Considering the appalling superstition of the Protestants and their naive dependence on signs and wonders, it was a strangely inconsistent stand. It was of course prompted by their hatred of Catholic "superstitions." But in those days there was little to choose between superstitions, as we are powerfully reminded when we read in the Puritan Baxter of such prodigies as "the drying up of the River Derwent in Darbyshire upon no known cause in winter, and the earth opening and swallowing a woman . . . upon her own imprecations." Alchemists and astrologers were summoned to Cromwell's camp by parliamentary order to come to the help of the Lord. The invasion of the supernatural was the familiar rule rather than the puzzling exception, and even Newton thought that God had to regulate minor irregularities in the solar system by personal intervention. Browne draws the line at only one type of miracles — Catholic relics, and his reason is characteristic. It is because he has so little respect for antiquities compared with the one antiquity — Eternity! In short then, he easily dismisses Bible miracles as unimportant. What may strike us as a sly skepticism is probably no more than the mere first glimmer of a spirit of scientific inquiry whose trend Browne himself scarcely recognizes and which really scarcely disturbs him. Such really giant infidels as Hobbes and Hume were yet to appear on the horizon.

He is not afraid of atheism. Indeed, he says, "I have been these many years of opinion there never was any. . . . That doctrine of Epicurus, that denied the providence of God, was no atheism, but a magnificent and high-strained conceit of his majesty, which he deemed too sublime to mind the trivial actions of those inferior creatures. That fatal necessity of the Stoics is nothing but the immutable law of his will." We remember from many passages that Bacon was not afraid of atheism either; he looked upon atheists with contempt as little-minded men: "It is true, that a little philosophy inclineth men's minds to atheism; but depth in philosophy bringeth men's minds about to religion. . . . Nay even that school which is most accused of atheism doth most demonstrate religion; that is the school of Leucippus and Democritus and Epicurus."[32] And he goes on to remark that contemplative atheists are rare.[33] Both men take the same ground: they look down from the majestic heights of what has proved to be the most workable argument for God, the teleological. It was the argument of the Deists and of Butler; Kant found a place for it and it is a respectable argument today. Browne indeed dismisses atheism with a certain rhetorical recklessness. Epicurus, the Stoics, any large philosophy, may be called theistic! This is certainly broad — too broad for a churchman who loves to "keep the road," too broad certainly for plain accuracy. But the intention is clear. Browne is simply making an impulsive protest against the rigid and confining definitions of contemporary theology.

Some years later Ralph Cudworth was to see this matter in a clearer light than anybody in Browne's generation. Neither the notions of "construction" nor of "evolution" involve or exclude God, he says at the outset of his *True Intellectual System*; these are merely the *process*. Atheism is to "acknowledge no other substance besides body or matter." And he distinguishes between Calvinism and Stoicism in a ruthless manner calculated to cut the Calvinists to the quick. Both are fatalism, he says, but Calvinism, which bases everything on the arbitrary will of God, is "divine fate *immoral*"; Stoicism, which believed in moral ideas

[32] "Of Atheism."
[33] Compare *Vulgar Errors*, I, x: "Many there are, who cannot conceive there was ever any absolute atheist, or such as could determine there was no God, without all check from himself, or contradiction from his other opinions."

and a Supreme Being but identified him with the invariable order of nature, is "divine fate *moral.*" Browne has no such clearcut ideas, but he thinks in the same direction. Toward the end of his life he advises his son Edward in a letter not to read Lucretius, "there being divers impieties in it."[34] He may have turned more conservative. But the passage in *Religio Medici* is certainly an evidence, if an impulsive one, of his refusal to shut out any large speculative truth.

VI

There is another interesting turn a little farther on in the book.[35] The subject of rabbinical interpretations of Scripture leads him to marvel at the strange obstinacy of "that contemptble and degenerate issue of Jacob." These are strong words for Browne, but he seems for once to have shared a contemporary prejudice; his gravely elaborate rejection of the current belief "That Jews Stink" in *Vulgar Errors* would scarcely mend matters. Yet he cannot help admiring their constancy: "The Jew is obstinate in all fortunes . . . they have suffered, in a bad cause, even to the condemnation of their enemies." And he feels strongly that the differences of religion are incompatible, that the lines are permanently drawn. It is the chameleon changes of Christians that astound him. All in all there is little hope of a religious union. And then he lays down a simple and direct principle: "Persecution is a bad and indirect way to plant religion."

He stands well ahead of his time here. It is true that he has nothing of the indignation of men like Chillingworth and Taylor against religious cruelty, but probably Fuller's remark that "even the mildest authors" agree that some heretics should be put to death is fairly representative, and Taylor's own unhappy resort to force against the Irish Presbyterians must not be forgotten. So insistent is Browne in his opposition to persecution that he utters some extravagant sentiments on the subject of martyrs.[36] This subject is a curious complex of his. There seems to be little question that he was naturally timid. We get hints of it in his scarcely concealed admiration of the Stoics' courage in facing suicide, a subject to which he recurs again and again; in

[34] *Works*, VI, 66. (Wilkin, III, 442.)
[35] *Religio Medici*, I, 25.
[36] *Ibid.*, I, 26.

his admiration of martyrs, especially old men who, though they "held up shaking hands in the fire," nevertheless "sit in the orchestra and noblest seats of heaven";[37] in the letter he wrote to his son Tom in the navy imploring him not to blow up the ship in case of defeat.[38] In the present passage in *Religio Medici* he extols martyrdom as the only true courage, and he says timidly and humbly, one feels with a personal application, that not everyone can have "so audacious and resolute a temper, as to endure those terrible tests and trials." He feels that something less is acceptable to God. And yet for all this his view of martyrdom suddenly takes a new turn. He becomes shrewd to the point of coldness. Not all men who die for religion are martyrs. He even attacks John Huss: some call him heretic, others martyr; it is doubtful, says Sir Thomas, if he was either. Many whose names are in martyrologies "in the eyes of God are not so perfect martyrs as was that wise heathen Socrates, that suffered on a fundamental point of religion, the unity of God." As for me, he declared, there are not many who "fear the face of death less than myself; yet, from the moral duty I owe to the commandment of God, and the natural respects that I tender unto the conservation of my essence and being, I would not perish upon a ceremony, politic points, or indifferency." "The leaven of all actions," in short, "is wisdom; without which to commit ourselves to the flames is homicide, and (I fear) but to pass through one fire into another."

All this is very interesting. The long and short of the matter is that Browne has no use for enthusiasts. From one point of view that solemn argument against useless suicide with its precious respect for his "essence and being" sounds suspiciously like Jack Falstaff on the field of honor, but from another angle it is the cool common sense of "Androcles and the Lion." These "root and branch" men might seem to some to be heroically "proud, calm, inflexible, sagacious"; to Browne they were stiff-necked egotists, and he damps their heroics and their martyr airs with the utmost coldness. He felt that England had had enough religious lunacy. Years later his sentiments crop out again in *Urn Burial* where he remarks quite gratuitously that "men have lost their reason in nothing so much as their religion, wherein stones

[37] *Urn Burial*, chap. iv.
[38] *Works*, VI, 23. (Wilkin, III, 417.)

and clouts make martyrs." [39] He has the contemptuous emotions of a Stoic sage in the face of a mad world. It comes out again in connection with scholars' disputes.[40] In all disputes, so much as there is of passion, so much there is of nothing to the purpose." "This is one reason why controversies are never determined," he says; men desert reason and never touch the question at issue. And he concludes impatiently, "The foundations of religion are already established, and the principles of salvation subscribed unto by all. There remain not many controversies worth a passion." Perhaps another sentence from these later pages sums up the whole case against zeal: "'Tis the general complaint of these times, and perhaps of those past, that charity grows cold; which I perceive most verified in those which do manifest the fires and flames of zeal; for it is a virtue that best agrees with coldest natures, and such as are complexioned for humility." [41]

But it is in the closing pages of the first part of the book that Browne's liberalism appears at its best. The question of salvation was the hard core of religious controversy. The complacent assumption was that each sect had the only valid passport, the one point of common agreement being that the heathen were damned. A few men like Hales protested that they would leave the church rather than not believe in the salvation of virtuous heathen, but they were in the minority. Browne is less bold than Hales and reluctantly accepts as an inscrutable mystery the damnation of the heathen, but he hates sectarian intolerance and for once speaks out plainly and with barbed contempt.

He begins with an orthodox pronouncement, but obviously it troubles him: "There is no salvation to those that believe not in Christ . . . which makes me much apprehend the end of those honest worthies and philosophers which died before his incarnation." [42] For a moment he goes on to consider this matter with a characteristic mixture of wistful musing, irony, and pious submission. "It is hard to place those souls in hell, whose worthy lives do teach us virtue on earth; methinks, amongst those many

[39] *Urn Burial*, chap. iv.
[40] *Religio Medici*, II, 3.
[41] *Ibid.*, II, 4.
[42] *Ibid.*, I, 54.

subdivisions of hell, there might have been one limbo left for these. . . . How strange to them will sound the history of Adam, when they shall suffer for him they never heard of!" But he falls back on the stock arguments of the inscrutable wisdom of God and the inadequacy of mere morality, and repeats his pious confession: "I do desire with God that all, but yet affirm with men that few, shall know salvation."

But here the tone changes. That "desire with God . . . but affirm with men" is the telling stroke. And from this point on he proceeds with a vigor and earnestness worthy of Hooker or Chillingworth or Taylor to expose the folly of exclusive pretension to salvation. Few shall be saved, "yet those who do confine the church of God either to particular nations, churches, or families, have made it far narrower than our Savior ever meant it." How absurd it is to "wrap the church of God in Strabo's cloak, and restrain it unto Europe. . . . 'Tis true, we all hold there is a number of elect, and many to be saved; yet take our opinions together, and from the confusion thereof, there will be no such thing as salvation, nor shall anyone be saved." Every church and sect excludes the other and "thus whilst the mercies of God do promise us heaven, our conceits and opinions exclude us from that place . . . and thus we go to heaven against each other's wills, conceits, and opinions. . . . The number of those who pretend unto salvation, and those infinite swarms who think to pass through the eye of this needle, have much amazed me. That name and compellation of little flock"—there is fine irony in this—"doth not comfort, but deject, my devotion; especially when I reflect upon mine own unworthiness. . . . It is beyond my ambition to aspire unto the first ranks; my desires only are, and I shall be happy therein, to be the last man, and bring up the rear in heaven. . . . Again, I am confident, and fully persuaded, yet dare not take my oath, of my salvation." It is true that we were elected from eternity, "and thus"—here is a characteristic flash of quaint imagination—"I was dead before I was alive; though my grave be England, my dying place was Paradise; and Eve miscarried of me before she conceived of Cain." Yet on the other hand, "insolent zeals that do decry good works and rely only upon faith, take not away merit: for, depending upon the efficacy of their faith, they enforce the condition of God, and in a more sophistical way do seem to challenge heaven. . . . I do not deny but that true faith . . . is a means of our salvation; but where to find this is as obscure to me as my last end . . . surely, that which we boast of is not anything, or, at the most, but a remove from nothing."

Quite clearly the charitable Sir Thomas Browne is capable of a measured and crushing controversial style. Years later the subject of the salvation of the heathen cropped up again, this time in a somewhat different light. He is admiring now not so much the virtue of the heathen as the dauntless courage with which they faced a possibility that was always terrible for Browne, the thought of annihilation. He condemns again and again, as though drawn to the subject by a secret and fascinated admiration, the fortitude with which the ancients contemplated suicide. And in *Urn Burial* this amazement finds expression in an astonishing passage that carries us from the martyrs seated in heaven to Epicurus lying in hell. The Christian martyrs, he thinks, are august and sublimely heroic beings, even the old men who though they "held up shaking hands in the fire" now "sit in the orchestra and noblest seats of heaven," but he seems by contrast to be lost in wonder at the courage of the pagan philosophers. He follows them in imagination to Dante's hell, that mighty embodiment of the Christian world-view. "Pythagoras escapes in the fabulous hell of Dante, among that swarm of philosophers, wherein whilst we meet with Plato and Socrates, Cato is to be found in no lower place than purgatory. Among all the set, Epicurus is most considerable, whom men make honest without an Elysium, who contemned life without encouragement of immortality, and making nothing after death, yet made nothing of the king of terrors." [43]

The picture strikes his imagination beyond bounds, and he throws it graphically upon a canvas that depicts the fate of the martyr and the pagan in one scene. In the upper half is the white-robed company of the elect. "Meanwhile Epicurus lies deep in Dante's hell, wherein we meet with tombs enclosing souls which denied their immortalities. But whether the virtuous heathen, who lived better than he spake, or erring in the principle of him-

---

[43] *Urn Burial*, chap. iv.

self, yet lived above philosophers of more specious maxims, lie so deep as he is placed, at least so low as not to rise against Christians, who believing or knowing that truth, have lastingly denied it in their practice and conversation, were a query too sad to insist on."[44] There is an extraordinary vividness in that "meanwhile." It conveys again that uncertain emotion — part dark brooding on the inscrutable wisdom that populates hell with the flower of the old civilization merely for the accident of being born before it, part ironic contrast. The company of martyrs looks a little smug and unadventurous. Browne has brought them too close to the Promethean figures of Epicurus, and Socrates "warming his doubtful spirits against that cold potion," and Cato "reading the Immortality of Plato" on the fateful night. Single-handed these redoubtable souls could face extinction — "the heaviest stone that melancholy can throw at a man." Browne takes refuge from that terrible thought in the protecting arms of Christian faith, but he looks back with obvious admiration to the brave pagans.

In this reluctance to believe in the damnation of the heathen Browne shares the growing ethical enlightenment of the Renaissance. Thoughtful men, reacting from the rigors of predestination, with its accompaniment of heaven and hell so confidently chartered by the elect, were bound to be struck by the fact that Christianity was not only as pessimistic and fatalistic as Stoicism, but less ethical and rational. In an age of harsh sectarian strife and theological crudity, the Stoic gravitation to ethics as a center, its emphasis on the harmony of nature, on cosmopolitan culture, on moral repose and equanimity, on moral freedom, its contempt for all but the wise man was highly congenial to many.

This Stoic contempt for the crowd comes near to the heart of the matter. Browne, for all his charity and freedom from antipathies, has one prejudice: he hates the multitude. "If there be any among those common objects of hatred I do contemn and laugh at, it is that great enemy of reason, virtue, and religion, the multitude; that numerous piece of monstrosity, which, taken asunder, seem men, and the reasonable creatures of God, but, confused together, make but one great beast, and a monstrosity

[44] *Ibid.*

more prodigious than Hydra."[45] And by multitude he means not simply the proletarian herd: "There is a rabble even amongst the gentry; a sort of plebeian heads . . . men in the same level with mechanics, though their fortunes do somewhat gild their infirmities, and their purses compound for their follies." And he goes on to contrast the "nobility without heraldry" of the primitive commonwealth with the "corruption of these times" when every one has a "liberty to amass and heap up riches and . . . to do or purchase anything." In other words the spectacle of English democracy in the making had turned Browne, as it had many of his generation, into something of a Stoic. He has retired from the tumult. He despises the whole tone of the society that was disintegrating the old social order, with its shifting standards of life, its fortune hunters, its political adventurers, and on the other hand its rising tide of raw plebeians with their uncouth religions and insolent political ambitions.

Perhaps the most violent language that Browne uses anywhere is to be found in this connection, in his chapter in *Vulgar Errors* dealing with The Erroneous Disposition of the People.[46] It reminds us of some of the furious invective of the *Anatomy of Melancholy*. A citation or two will suffice. "Their individual imperfections being great, they are moreover enlarged by their aggregation; and being erroneous in their single numbers, once huddled together, they will be Error itself. For being a confusion of knaves and fools, and a farraginous concurrence of all conditions, tempers, sexes, and ages; it is but natural if their determinations be monstrous, and many ways inconsistent with truth." And then he proceeds to pay his respects to the venerable *vox populi vox Dei*: "Certainly he that considereth these things . . . will easily discern how little of truth there is in the ways of the multitude; and though sometimes they are flattered with that aphorism, will hardly believe, The voice of the people to be the voice of God." Whoever, finally, shall resign their reasons to popular opinions "although their condition and fortunes may place them many spheres above the multitude, yet are they still within the line of vulgarity, and democratical enemies of truth." Bacon had recently said the same thing: "The master of super-

[45] *Religio Medici*, II, 1.
[46] *Vulgar Errors*, I, iii.

stition is the people; and in all superstition wise men follow fools." Hooker might seem to contradict it in his famous dictum that "the general and perpetual voice of men is as the voice of God himself," but it all comes to the same thing. All these men believe in the wisdom of great minds, seasoned and tested by institutions, and they stand together against the democratic upheaval.

They represent, in fact, the moderate Anglican position, essentially Protestant, and opposed at definite points both to the extreme High Churchmen and the extreme Puritans. Browne's position, with the differences that have been noted, is theirs. He accepts the Bible, he accepts the church, he accepts the right of private judgment. This involved complications no more resolved by him than by any of his contemporaries. He did not have the unifying grasp of Hooker, the sharp, statesmanlike directness of Falkland or Chillingworth, the scientific advantage of Bacon's tight, compartmental attitude, yet Browne had endowments that these others lacked. His mind was not so clear or so boldly constructive as theirs, but many readers will feel that it was a richer mind. However that may be, it was compounded of violently opposite and paradoxical traits. The seventeenth century, in the nature of the case, produced extraordinarily complex men. The Puritans themselves, with their stark mixture of self-abasement and pride, fatalistic despair and capacity for practical action, outward freedom and inward compulsion, are the best examples of these picturesque and bizarre combinations. In a very different way Browne is equally paradoxical. Shrinking from the fierce light of the Puritans' awful, transcendent, irrational God and their rigid scheme of salvation which paralyzes his imagination and shrivels his moral nature, he retreats sometimes into the Gothic shadow of the church where he may see God through the veil of dogma, sometimes into the great reaches of free philosophical speculation, sometimes into the smallest and hidden haunts of nature where he may feel him immanent in the world, and these aspects of metaphysics, science and poetry he combines in that many-colored and paradoxical personality which is, after all is said, his indiscerptible self.

How can we sum up his religious qualities? He combines the believer and the skeptic, the acute intellect and the propensity to faith. He makes a synthesis which is the result partly of tolerance, and the ability to see both sides at once, partly of a lack of power to formulate general principles, and of a great overweight of learning. He has that rational conservatism which is characteristic of English Protestantism. It involves a confidence in the superiority of the intellectual and broadly cultured man to popular aberrations. It involves besides in Browne's case a certain isolation, due partly perhaps to timidity, partly to his Stoic reserve and fastidious withdrawal from violence and irrational "enthusiasm." His is the strength of a powerful, solitary mind, always sensitively aware of the order and structure of the world and always alive to its spiritual meaning.

In this respect Browne's *Religio Medici* points ahead, for it is practically contemporaneous with the publication of Descartes' first great work, the *Discours de la Méthode*. The Cartesian separation of matter and mind reset the philosophic stage and its impact upon England was almost immediate. At the same time Hobbes was developing his system of pure materialism, and his *Leviathan* (1651) ruthlessly applied its principles to psychology and political economy. The issues raised by Descartes and Hobbes led to a re-examination of the foundations of religious philosophy, particularly at the hands of the Cambridge Platonists. It was opposition to both the Hobbesian and Calvinist determinism that lead the Cambridge Platonists, as indeed Milton, to reassert free will and the humanist and Christian doctrine of right reason. In the face of the new mechanic philosophy, the object of the Cambridge Platonists was to put God back into the world, and to find a place, and a primary place, for the conception of spirit. Browne leans toward this later movement, and in his philosophical perceptions and sympathies provides a kind of link between Hooker and the Cambridge Platonists. The next chapter will consider him in these relations.

CHAPTER III

The Art of God

I

THE philosophy of Sir Thomas Browne lies within the framework of knowledge and beliefs that was inherited from the Middle Ages and carried down through the Renaissance in the long tradition of Christian humanism. This world-view with its divinely constituted order, harmony, and proportion, was as common in all its essentials to Shakespeare and Milton as to Thomas Aquinas, to Martin Luther as to Richard Hooker. The divine order extended in a great chain or ladder of being from top to bottom of the universe.

"There is in this universe," Browne himself says, "a stair or manifest scale of creatures, rising not disorderly or in confusion, but with a comely method and proportion. Between creatures of mere existence, and things of life, there is a large disproportion of nature; between plants, and animals or creatures of sense, a wider difference; between them and man, a far greater; and if the proportion hold on, between man and angels there should be yet a greater."[1]

Browne's conception of the scale of being is altogether different from ours. He is thinking in terms of the moral excel-

[1] *Religio Medici*, I, 33.

lence of minerals, vegetables, and animals, and their exact gradation in every kind and species, of the levels of the elements, of celestial spheres, of spirits, good and bad, of intelligences, affinities, and sympathies, of the hierarchies of angels and their various attributes and duties, and of man as the unique meeting place of matter and spirit.

The pattern of this vast system, the complexity of which it is impossible to suggest here, has now been broken. Teleology has no place in modern science, and the traditional body of knowledge is unfamiliar to us now except in detached fragments of old lore, picked up perhaps in footnotes to Elizabethan plays, or to *Paradise Lost,* or in the astrological chart in an almanac. The old science had long shown signs of decay, but the beginning of the end was at hand, if a decisive point may be chosen, when Bacon excluded theology from his scientific program. It is clear that he intended merely to mark off a workable territory for empirical investigation; within the limitations of his character and interests Bacon was far from irreligious, and he nobly proclaimed the idea moral and religious ends of science. But he does not prevent the question arising as to whether his system of natural science really permits a religious interpretation of the world. At all events, his separation of revealed knowledge from human knowledge, orthodox though it was, pointed to the path that science was to take. By stages God was relegated to another sphere and eventually pushed out of the phenomenal world altogether.

This was for the future. To the seventeenth-century man, the world of present-day science, stripped of moral purpose, as of color and sound, its ultimate reality reduced to the mathematical abstractions of vibrating atomic patterns, would be meaningless. He did not think of himself as a helpless onlooker, and certainly not as a mere machine. His universe was informed to its very core with the purpose of its creator and man himself was crowned with glory and honor. The harmony of this order was marred by the defection of the rebel angels and the sin of man, but the divine plan embraced evil also and turned it to good.

The tradition of Christian humanism was based, of course, on biblical theology. The Mosaic cosmogony, in which God made the world in six days and breathed into man a unique soul, was binding on the authority of Scripture. The resultant theology involved a transcendent creator and a manufactured world, produced in time and out of nothing. It kept matter and spirit, natural and supernatural, sharply apart in a thoroughgoing dualism. In spite of this dominantly simple point of view, however, Christianity was always complex, and seventeenth-century Christianity, wavering as it did between decaying Scholasticism and the new assertions of science, reached in the effort a new stage of complexity. Any one of Sir Thomas Browne's books is a fruitful illustration of what happened when the primitive Jewish theology was combined with the highly speculative systems of Greek philosophy, and when all this in turn was accommodated to new ideas from time to time. There have been three great historical theories about the origin of the phenomenal world: first, that it is a pure mechanism; second, that it springs from the fecund and creative power of nature; third, that it was made by an intelligent creator. As John Tyndall says,[2] pure scientists are content with the first view, analytic minds combine the first and third, and those of synthetic temperament who have lofty feelings and ethical cravings, combine the second and third in various ways, being either pantheists or believers in some form of the doctrine of immanence. Seventeenth-century philosophy, rich in speculative tradition as it was, produced every possible combination of these theories.

First, there was Platonism. Platonic philosophy in its various aspects has always influenced Christianity in many and incalculable directions, and not least in the Renaissance. Because of its own double nature, Platonic idealism has tended partly to support, partly to resolve, the dualism of Christian metaphysics. On one side Platonism is dualistic, for it separates the world of sense from the world of true being, the real from the non-real, the pattern from the copy. On the other side it is monistic, for it holds that the many, though separate, are immanent in the One, and that the unreal and ephemeral find a being in the Changeless. Spenser and Milton are the great English exemplars of Christian Platonism in the Renaissance. Plato is everywhere

[2] "Address" delivered before the British Association assembled at Belfast, in *British Association for the Advancement of Science*, Report 44th, 1874 (London, 1875).

in Milton, and in spite of the rigid, dogmatic framework of *Paradise Lost* and some arid theological exposition, there is a Platonic light about its doctrines that transforms most of them into poetry. This fusion of Christianity and Platonism is still more marked in Spenser. His four hymns illustrate how indifferently he uses now Venus, now the Logos to express his philosophy of beauty. In the "Hymn in Honor of Love," Venus is the great mother, and Love the "Great God of Might." By her light he moves through chaos, compounding the four elements of the world, whose fertility is due to the "secret sparks of his infused fire." In the "Hymn of Heavenly Love," Spenser easily changes to the theme of

> That high eternal Power, which now doth move
> In all these things, mov'd in itself by love

and goes on to celebrate the Christian story of the redemption. Finally, in the "Hymn of Heavenly Beauty" he makes beauty the inclusive name for the Absolute, for that Eternal Truth and Sapience

> Whose beauty fills the heavens with her light,
> And darks the earth with shadow of her sight.

But this is only one aspect of Spenser's philosophy. Though he goes to Plato for his ideal of changeless perfection, he will not say with him that matter is unreal or evil or dead. He has the instinct which poets share with biologists that nature is a creative power, that, as Bruno said, "Nature is not the mere empty capacity which philosophers have pictured, but the fruitful universal mother." In this hylozoism, to give it a technical name, he deserts Plato for Aristotle, Lucretius, and Bruno. According to a famous passage in *The Fairy Queen*,[3] matter, not idea, is eternal, and life and soul are in each atom. The symbol of this philosophy is the garden of Adonis, of which Venus is the mystical patron and Old Genius the porter. This is the "first seminary" of Dame Nature, and here all things are born out of primal matter in nature's womb:

> All things from thence do their first being fetch,
> And borrow matter whereof they are made,

[3] III. vi. 29 ff.

Which, whenas form and feature it does ketch,
Becomes a body, and doth then invade
The state of life out of the griesly shade.
That substance is eterne, and bideth so,
Ne when the life decays, and form does fade
Doth it consume and into nothing go,
But chaunged is, and often altered to and fro.

The words "mind" and "matter" have suffered countless vicissitudes in the history of thought. Thomas Aquinas had settled the matter temporarily for theology; as a moderate realist, he held that matter was real, and the principle of individuation but created in time. As a poet Spenser has a very old and persistent instinct. His mind reaches farther back and perhaps farther forward than the dogmatic decisions of the Church. He has a feeling that nature is a plastic and eternal force, a feeling which he derives partly from the biological instincts of the Greeks, partly from the new spirit of his own day. But like Bruno, he finds it easy to combine this idea with the conception of an immanent God. Milton in *Paradise Lost* makes the same combination. So in their own way do the Cambridge Platonists and Sir Thomas Browne. The result was a half-reconciled dualism between God and nature.

One way to avoid this dualism, which lies so deep in Platonic and Christian metaphysics, had long been provided by the mystical, pantheistic philosophies of the Neo-Platonists, evolved out of Platonism by the Greek and Jewish schools of Alexandria. How, they asked, can the gap between God and the world be bridged? How can Infinity create the finite? How can the Absolute and the Changeless be altered or added to? And Philo, Plotinus, and their followers answered the question in the same way: The Infinite and the Changeless cannot create; the world is not a creation, but an emanation, and matter is a distant, pale, weakened beam from the unknowable, invisible source of eternal light. This oriental idealism was never congenial to the solid, teleological Christianity of the West, but it often found lodgment there and supplied a mystical strain. In Jewish theology it developed down through the Middle Ages into the exotic mysticism of the Cabbala. In the Renaissance Neo-Platonism was revived by Ficino, Pico della Mirandola, and other mystical

Platonists. Much of the Platonism of the period came through Neo-Platonic channels, and the Cabbala deeply influenced Christian thought.

Side by side with these philosophies, and indeed an offspring of them, was the ancient tradition of the occult sciences, especially alchemy and astrology, with their secret formulas, their white and black magic, their potent symbols, their "sympathies" that bound phenomena together, their cosmic levels, their attendant demons and spirits, their short cuts to the hidden heart of nature. This was a territory in which Browne was more or less at home and it will be impossible to understand him without at least straying into the borders of it. Every one then, from Bacon to Boyle, felt the lingering excitement of the quest which these mystrious sciences undertook — to unlock nature's secrets by magic formulas. In the case of alchemy a certain cult, toward which Browne was at least sympathetic, had sublimated the search for the philosopher's stone into an elaborate religious symbolism more or less vaguely connected with Christianity. The Rosicrucians represented the tendency, and there were other varieties of the same sort of thing. These Hermetic philosophies of one kind and another were still to be reckoned with, and men of romantic turn were still partly under their spell, and might with Il Penseroso

> oft out-watch the Bear,
> With thrice great Hermes, or unsphere
> The spirit of Plato to unfold
> What worlds, or what vast regions hold
> The immortal mind that hath forsook
> Her mansion in this fleshly nook:
> And of those Daemons that are found
> In fire, air, flood, or underground,
> Whose power hath a true consent
> With planet, or with element.

Scholastic Christianity was, however, predominantly Aristotelian, and the orthodox natural philosophy, as the handmaiden of theology, based its whole authority and method on Aristotle. Since this great name bulks so large in Browne's writings it will do no harm to dwell for a moment on the familiar truth that

Aristotelianism as the Middle Ages knew it was very different from Aristotle. It was the Aristotelian biology and logic as modified by medieval philosophy that launched the Middle Ages on its barren search for abstract principles, static forms, and final causes. But Aristotelianism was a very different thing from the real teachings of the Greek philosopher.

Aristotle's famous "entelechy," or "form," was the chief stumbling block for the Middle Ages. But the Scholastics were not altogther to blame for their confusion. For Aristotle himself was certainly inconsistent. It is uncertain whether he believed in an external God or in an internal principle of life in nature, and his doctrine of the soul is thoroughly confused. The Middle Ages had to make what groping use they could of these conceptions. We find Bacon and Browne, for instance, divided, the former blaming Aristotle for his dominant concern with final causes, which led him to mix physics and theology, the latter blaming him for neglecting final causes. We find Cudworth linking Plato and Aristotle together as believers in the world soul. There is unquestionable ground for these various interpretations.

Aristotle is really a biologist, the founder of systematic zoology, and if the Middle Ages had studied the phenomenal world and thought of nature in terms of evolutionary development, they could have found the germs of science in his works. He almost seems, at times, to recognize the method of nature. He sees, as few seventeenth-century biologists did, that the mole's eyes are congenitally arrested. He is on the edge of tracing a progress from inanimate to animate.

But only the germs of these ideas are in Aristotle. For his system is strangely confused, mingling the elements of an external creator, and an internal dynamic force, and a soul which is a strangely compounded monstrosity. Furthermore, the world, as he conceived it, is static and immutable. Above all, we cannot tell whether he thinks of nature as a single force or an assemblage of forces, whether as something independent, or an emanation from the divine activity. There is no question that his universe is teleological through and through, but though he conceives nature to be a single force with an all-efficient purpose, he cannot work out the idea consistently. He fails, in short, to solve the opposition between physical and final causes, or to explain how body and soul are united, and thus he is unable to overcome that fundamental dualism which is so characteristic of Greek philosophy.

Scholasticism was still less in a position to overcome this dualism. It added little to Aristotle's knowledge of physics and biology — indeed he was in advance of the seventeenth century in many ways — and it thought in still more strictly teleological terms. But it used Aristotle's logical apparatus and accommodated the Greek physics, biology, and psychology to Christian orthodox doctrines. The Scholastic philosophers made dialectic use of the four Aristotelian "causes" and of his "form" to explain the operations of God in nature and the relations of soul and body. They accepted the classical divisions of the soul and at the same time insisted on its unity. They carried into Christianity the Greek notion that nature was animate. Thus they tried to unify the world by a hybrid theory which posited a manufactured world and a transcendent creator on the one hand, and animate nature on the other. They believed in the theory of special creation and of spontaneous generation — an ancient doctrine which they were compelled to call in to account for the myriad forms of life whose existence constituted a growingly embarrassing mystery. Thus science was deadlocked. It was concerned mainly with final causes in a theoretically static world. But the theory obviously did not fit, and it was hopelessly tangled with complications. With none but logical, highly abstract methods of studying nature, and thinking of phenomena as locked into fixed patterns, they were completely helpless. It was impossible for them to make any new discoveries about the phenomenal world.

All this confusion is shown clearly in Bacon. Bacon's grand program was to turn his back on the past two thousand years and to begin the unification of knowledge by an entirely new method. He proposes first to overthrow Aristotelianism and turn from logic to nature herself. His method is to set theology to one side, and confine his attention to natural philosophy, for he sees clearly that the introduction by the Socratic schools of the question of teleology, under the dominance of their interest in the soul, had interrupted and hopelessly complicated scientific knowledge. "The inquisition of final causes is barren, and like a virgin consecrated to God, produces nothing," he says in a famous sentence. And so he passes over Plato and Aristotle and returns to the early Greek atomists. He formally acknowledges the truth of revealed religion, but he insists on the separation of physics and metaphysics. So in the *Advancement of Learning* he marks out clearly the limits of nature study: it cannot prove more than the existence of God. It can certainly prove this, for Bacon is a believer in teleology, but it can prove no more; nature is simply the *work* of God. On this basis he proceeds to erect his new method.

But we see immediately to what an extent he still thinks in the old terms. Though he exposes the syllogistic method with crushing force, showing how blind and clumsy an instrument it is, and how helpless before the subtlety of nature, yet his own inductive experiment lacks modern method and imaginative insight. He is still looking for the clue to "forms" in a very vague, Aristotelian way. His world is only half unified by law; thinking in terms of freaks and supernatural invasions, he speaks of "hounding nature in her wanderings." He still believes that all bodies have a "soul" or animating principle and a diffused sensation, and though he rejects such Aristotelian and scholastic metaphors as *natura nihil facit frustra, omnis res fugit sui destructionem, similia similibus gaudent,* because, as he says, they put nature in the place of God, nevertheless he cannot rid his mind of these ideas, and we find him speaking of the *motus nexus* which makes bodies delight in contact and refuse to be separated, and of cream rising because of the desire of the elements for each other. These notions are the warp and woof of his intellectual world and he cannot think himself free from them.

Yet Bacon was considerably in advance of his time. Browne needs to be studied in connection with him, because Bacon vigorously exposes so many of the philosophical weaknesses of which Browne was a signal victim, and at the same time shares so many. Both illustrate the defects of the generation which almost closes with Browne: they show the inertia, if not paralysis, of a world waiting for the scientific method to be born. They are alike in rejecting some of the greatest discoveries of the day. And they are alike in another way. Bacon of course did much for science, but like Browne, he was primarily a man of letters. Their point of view was totally different: to the one "Knowledge is power" and "Wonder is but broken knowledge"; to the other *Lux est umbra Dei* and "Nature is the art of God"; but from these antipodes of philosophical outlook, each is an imaginative mind flashing in the dark.

One other phase of thought needs to be touched on in this introductory survey. It reached its height only in Browne's last years, and he nowhere indicates that he was aware of its existence, but he seems spiritually closer to it than to any other movement. That is the school of the Cambridge Platonists. In the years in which Browne was writing *Religio Medici* Descartes had suddenly appeared. His epistemology and his dualistic world of extension and mind, distinguished with crystal simplicity and mathematical bareness, provided the method that inaugurated modern philosophy. Browne was certainly aware of Descartes by 1646, on the evidence of his citations in *Vulgar Errors*, and since Browne's philosophy of nature receives further elaboration in *Vulgar Errors* and *The Garden of Cyrus*, it is of interest to measure it alongside the Cartesian philosophy and that English school of theology which definitely reacted from Descartes.

The Cambridge Platonists were the successors of Hooker. They carried on his teaching—that religion is a life and a spirit and that it is fundamentally rational. But they were compelled to examine their principles in the light of the new mechanic philosophy and, in so doing, to find if possible a more satisfactory explanation of the relation of mind to matter than the one offered by orthodox teleological doctrines. Hobbes as a thoroughgoing materialist was their *bête noir,* and eventually they attacked Cartesianism itself. At first under More's leadership, they had hailed Descartes with enthusiasm, but in the end his philosophy, though they did not consider it ultimately incompatible with religion, proved to be too bare, too baldy dualistic to suit them. They could not accept the notion that the universe is a mechanical machine wound up to go on its own principles; they wanted to keep God and spirit at the center of the world. But neither, on the other hand, could they any longer believe that God directly intervenes in every process of nature, for they saw that this cannot explain nature's slow processes, her delays and mistakes. To solve their difficulties, they reintroduced the Platonic doctrine of plastic nature, a principle which they at first interpreted in terms of Descartes, but which later became in their hands a protest against the whole mechanic philosophy as they understood it.

The movement was confined to a small group of men in Emmanuel and Christ's Colleges, Cambridge, a Puritan stronghold, who under the popular nickname of "latitude men" spread their ideas in their sermons and philosophical writings, during the last days of the Commonwealth and the first decade of the Restoration. They were accused of teaching a kind of "moral divinity." Their general point of view, as it developed in one form or another in Benjamin Whichcote, Nathanael Culverwel, Henry More, and Ralph Cudworth, is that the divine intelligence and the spiritual world are supreme, that spirit is "senior," not "junior," and that God enters the world through the mediation of a kind of plastic soul in nature.

Culverwel says: "Why bodies only should engross and monopolize natural philosophy, and why a soul cannot be admitted into it . . . is a thing altogether unaccountable. . . . Herein Plato was defective that he did not correct and reform the abuse of this word nature; that he did not screw it up to a higher and more spiritual notion. For it is very agreeable to the eternal and supremest Being. Nature is that regular line which the wisdom of God Himself has drawn in being."[4] Aristotle is wrong, he says, to define nature as the principle of motion and rest. Nature is "the genius of entity, nay 'tis Being itself. There is no moment in which you can imagine a thing to be and yet to be without its nature. It is a principle of working in spirituals as well as *principium motus et quietis* in corporeals." In other words, he is looking for some new definition of mind and matter which will avoid dualism, which will include nature in a great order embracing both the spiritual and the material.

More carries on the same idea. "The primordials of the world," he says, "are not mechanical, but spermatical or vital . . . which some modern writers call the spirit of nature."[5] The world is not mere extension and thought: spirit is extended too, and it is more than thought: it is activity and will. So he unites spirit

[4] *Discourse of the Light of Nature* (1652).
[5] *Divine Dialogues*, Third Series (1668).

and matter under some such conception as the modern notion of force; spirit is activity. And he uses the ever powerful argument against materialism that matter might "grind itself into the more rude and general delineations of nature, but it fails wholly to account for the diversities of animal species. . . . How is it possible that any particle of matter, or many together . . . can have the idea impressed of the creature they are to frame?"[6] There must be, then, he thinks, a world soul "without sense and animadversion, pervading the whole matter of the universe, and exercising a plastical power therein."[7]

The fullest exposition of this theory of plastic nature is given by Cudworth in his massive work, *The True Intellectual System of the Universe*, which he brought out in 1672. His ideas in briefest form are these. The fundamental question is, What is the nature of the primal activity? Is it material or spiritual? Is mind "senior" or "junior"? Theories about the *process* are secondary. Neither a mechanistic nor an evolutionary theory affects religion; atheism is "to acknowledge no other substance besides body or matter." He admits the Greek systems as imperfect theism. But neither pure materialism nor hylozoism can explain the world, for a stupid or unconscious nature could not have evolved it. This is above all true of human personality, for certainly it could never spring out of "a heap of innumerable percipients and innumerable perceptions and intellections." "That which understandeth in us is an incorporeal soul." It follows then that "mind is senior to the world, and the architect thereof." But how do mind and nature interact? By plastic nature, which is "an inferior and subordinate instrument drudgingly executing that part of Providence which consists in the regular and orderly motion of matter — yet, so as there is besides a higher Providence which, presiding over it, doth often supply the defects of it, and sometimes overrule it — for as much as this plastic nature cannot act electively or with discretion." In other words, he says, unless we accept this notion of plastic nature we must either deny any God at all, or believe that God makes "every gnat and fly, insect and mite" with his own hands. Descartes seemed to him to push God out of the world, but the old teleol-

[6] *Antidote against Atheism*, Bk. II, chap. i.
[7] *Immortality of the Soul*, Bk. III, chap. xii.

ogy on the other hand brought him into it too naively. For if God is omnipotent he would do his work "infallibly and irresistibly" and it is obvious that nature's processes are full of "errors and bungles." There must be an intermediate agent, a plastic nature, and he defines it as "reason immersed and plunged into matter, and, as it were, fuddled in it and confounded with it." In effect, there is a virtual return in these thinkers to Plato's world soul — a dull power, recalcitrant and only half-conscious, through which the creator has to work out his purpose as best he can.

These in brief are the currents of thought which chiefly influenced Sir Thomas Browne's views about nature. As far as science is concerned, they belonged to a dying age. The seeds of the future were in the new experimental method, in the revival of the atomic theory, in the mathematical physics of Galileo, Kepler, and Newton, in the physiological discoveries of Harvey, and the isolated but bold researches in magnetism, chemistry, and biology.

II

The purpose of this preliminary sketch has been to set off a striking epigram of Sir Thomas Browne. He wrote it perhaps in 1635 or 1636, but it would have served quite as well for the motto of *The Garden of Cyrus* in 1658. The task here is to explore its meaning in the whole context of his books, and if possible trace out, through the symbols and imagery which he uses, those conceptions and intuitions which he cannot fully express, but which do not quite elude his greatest words.

"Nature is the art of God," he wrote at the close of the sixteenth section of *Religio Medici*. Whatever the ultimate source of this saying may be,[8] Hobbes used it later at the beginning of his *Leviathan*. It occurs again in an old pamphlet that announces the new Cambridge Platonist movement.[9] A certain "S. P. of Cambridge" describes there the revolt from Aristotle to the mechanic philosophy of Descartes, and makes a plea for the reunion of the

[8] Dante says (*De Monarchia*, II. Cap. 2): "Whatever good is in lesser things . . . must come first from the artist, God, and secondly from the instrument of divine art, heaven, which men generally call Nature." (. . . *organum . . . artis divinae, quam Naturam communiter appellant.*)

[9] "A Brief Account of the New Sect of Latitude-Men," etc., 1662. Published in *The Phoenix*, 1707.

Church of England and the Platonic philosophy, "her old loving nurse." "Nor is there any cause to doubt," he goes on to say, "but the mechanic also will be faithful to her, no less against the open violence of atheism, than the secret treachery of enthusiasm and superstition." He ridicules the meaningless jargon of the Scholastics about forms and qualities, and asks whether it is better philosophy to say that nature makes the fire burn than to say that art makes the clock strike. "For as art is to the artificials, so is nature to naturals; and may be he spake more truly than he was aware of that called it *ars Dei*," for surely the business of philosophy is "to find out the process of this divine art in the great automaton of the world . . . from the first springs or plummets, as I may say, to the hand that points out the visible and last effects."

Here is an epigram, "Nature is the art of God," that can cover the views of three writers as different as Browne, Hobbes, and a Cambridge Platonist. Taking it as a starting point, the problem is to find out what Browne meant by it. Certainly the light which his writings throw on this question casts a good many shadows. It has nothing of the intense glare of Calvinism, or the clarity of Descartes, and it lacks the common sense and utilitarian directness of Bacon. It is nearer to the idealism of the Cambridge Platonists, but it lacks their systematic grasp. If, on the other hand, it has mystical elements, these are guarded by a constant intellectual activity. But this activity is not long sustained or pushed far enough to crystallize into systems.

So here, as in other aspects of Browne's thought, it will be found best to indicate the direction rather than the logical limitation of his ideas. In the last analysis we may be assured he will elude us; there will be a protean change of thought into a symbol or a blinding paradox or an unanswered question and the pursuer is left standing. We soon come to two conclusions — that his metaphysical powers are fairly moderate, but that his imaginative range is really great and calls for the highest creative criticism.

In *Religio Medici,* the core of the discussion about nature is in Part I, sections 14 to 18. But it is characteristic of him that he approaches his formal statement of theological first principles, that "there is but one first cause, and four second causes of all things," by many a shadowy way and shorter wheeling flight. We have already touched upon these early passages where Browne's "haggard reason" stoops to the lure of faith, or loses itself in Trismegistus' mystical circle or the darkness of God's light, as he turns his thoughts upon the Trinity or upon the attributes of endless existence and power. Here he reveals at once his fixed predilection for symbolism. To him "this visible world is but a picture of the invisible," and he approaches nature only half convinced of its real existence; it may be only a counterfeit of "some real substance in that invisible fabric."

Only after these mystical flights does he come for a while to solid ground. "These are contemplations metaphysical: my humble speculations have another method, and are content to trace and discover those expressions he hath left in his creatures, and the obvious effects of nature. There is no danger to profound these mysteries, no *sanctum sanctorum* in philosophy." But we notice at once that he fixes the end of knowledge in true medieval fashion: "The world was made to be inhabited by beasts, but studied and contemplated by man: 'tis the debt of our reason we owe unto God." And then with quaint gravity he remarks that "the wisdom of God receives small honor from those vulgar heads that rudely stare about, and with a gross rusticity admire his works"; rather do we owe him "the duty of a devout and learned admiration." The thought is reminiscent of a passage in the *Utopia* where More thinks that "an exact and curious observer, who admires his workmanship is much more acceptable to him than one of the herd." Here then at the outset is the little world of the Middle Ages, almost as neat as Noah's ark, a cabinet of rarities, as Drummond calls it, with a divine showman to draw back the curtain. And Browne throws the ideas naively into one of those fragments of verse that intersperse his prose occasionally.

All this is simply preparatory to the sections that now follow, in which he attempts a serious exposition of the principles of natural philosophy. It is important to quote three of them in full:

"14. There is but one first cause, and four second causes of all things. Some are without efficient, as God; others without matter, as angels; some without form, as the first matter: but every essence, created or uncreated, hath its final cause, and some positive end, both of its essence and operation. This is the cause I grope after in the works of nature; on this hangs the providence of God. To raise so beauteous a structure as the world and the creatures thereof, was but his art; but their sundry and divided operations, with their predestinated ends, are from the treasure of his wisdom. In the causes, nature and affections of the eclipses of the sun and moon, there is most excellent speculation; but to profound farther, and to contemplate a reason why his providence hath so disposed and ordered their motions in that vast circle as to conjoin and obscure each other, is a sweeter piece of reason, and a diviner point of philosophy. Therefore sometimes and in some things, there appears to me as much divinity in Galen his books *De Usu Partium*, as in Suarez' metaphysics. Had Aristotle been as curious in the enquiry of this cause as he was of the other, he had not left behind him an imperfect piece of philosophy, but an absolute tract of divinity.

"15. *Natura nihil agit frustra,* is the only indisputed axiom in philosophy. There are no grotesques in nature; not anything framed to fill up empty cantons, and unnecessary spaces. In the most imperfect creatures and such as were not preserved in the ark, but, having their seeds and principles in the womb of nature, are everywhere, where the power of the sun is, in these is the wisdom of his hand discovered. Out of this rank Solomon chose the object of his admiration. Indeed what reason may not go to school to the wisdom of bees, ants, and spiders? What wise hand teacheth them to do what reason cannot teach us? Ruder heads stand amazed at those prodigious pieces of nature, whales, elephants, dromedaries, and camels; these, I confess, are the colossus and majestic pieces of her hand: but in these narrow engines there is more curious mathematics; and the civility of these little citizens more neatly sets forth the wisdom of their Maker. Who admires not Regio Montanus his fly beyond his eagle, or wonders not more at the operation of two souls in those little bodies than but one in the trunk of a cedar? I could never content my contemplation with those general pieces of wonder, the flux and reflux of the sea, the increase of Nile, the conversion of the needle to the north; and have studied to match and parallel those in the more obvious and neglected pieces of nature, which without further travel I can do in the cosmography of myself. We carry with us the wonders we seek without us: there is all Africa and her prodigies in us; we are that bold and adventurous piece of nature, which he that studies wisely learns in a compendium what others labor at in a divided piece and endless volume.

"16. Thus there are two books from whence I collect my divinity; besides that written one of God, another of his servant nature, that universal and public manuscript, that lies expansed unto the eyes of all: those that never saw him in the one, have discovered him in the other. This was the scripture and theology of the heathens: the natural motion of the sun made them more admire him than its supernatural station did the children of Israel; the ordinary effects of nature wrought more admiration in them than in the other all his miracles. Surely the heathens knew better how to join and read these mystical letters than we Christians, who cast a more careless eye on these common hieroglyphics, and disdain to suck divinity from the flowers of nature. Nor do I so forget God as to adore the name of nature; which I define not, with the schools, to be the principle of motion and rest, but that straight and regular line, that settled and constant course the wisdom of God hath ordained the actions of his creatures, according to their several kinds. To make a revolution every day is the nature of the sun, because of that necessary course which God hath ordained it, from which it cannot swerve but by a faculty from that voice which first did give it motion. Now this course of nature God seldom alters or perverts, but, like an excellent artist, hath so contrived his work, that with the self-same instrument, without a new creation, he may effect his obscurest designs. Thus he sweeteneth the water with a wood, preserveth the creatures in the ark, which the blast of his mouth might have as easily created; for God is like a skilful geometrician, who, when more easily and with one stroke of his compass he might describe or divide a right line, had yet rather do this in a circle or longer way, according to the constituted and forelaid principles of his art. Yet this rule of his he doth sometimes pervert, to acquaint the world with his prerogative, lest the arrogancy of our reason should question his power, and conclude he could not. And thus I call the effects of nature the works of God, whose hand and instrument she only is; and therefore to ascribe his actions unto her, is to devolve the honor of the principal agent upon the instrument; which if with reason we may do, then let our hammers rise up and boast they have built our houses, and our pens receive the honor of our writings. I hold there is a general beauty in the works of God, and therefore no deformity in any kind or species of creature whatsoever. I cannot tell by what logic we call a toad, a bear, or an elephant ugly; they being created in those outward shapes and figures which best express the actions of their inward forms, and having passed that general visitation of God, who saw that all that he had made was good, that is, conformable to his will, which abhors deformity, and is the rule of order and beauty. There is no deformity but in monstrosity; wherein, notwithstanding, there is a kind of beauty, nature so ingeniously contriving the irregular parts, as they become sometimes more remarkable than the principal fabric. To speak yet more narrowly, there was never anything ugly or misshapen, but the chaos; wherein, notwithstanding, to speak strictly, there was no deformity, because no form; nor was it yet impregnate by the voice of God. Now nature is not at variance with art, nor art with nature, they being both servants of his Providence. Art is the perfection of nature. Were the world now as it was the sixth day, there were yet a chaos. Nature hath made one world, and art another. In brief, all things are artificial; for nature is the art of God."

This is exceptionally interesting. But delightful territory though it is from the literary point of view, from the scientific it presents a somewhat rough and broken ground. As one ponders, however, on the connotations of its words, and phrases, certain of them stand out from the rest, some for their familiar Scholastic ring, others either for their strangeness or arresting original force. These terms are freighted with metaphysical cargoes, but quite clearly they come from many different ports, and it is with a feeling of romantic strangeness that we see them riding at anchor in one hospitable harbor.

The argument begins with a perfect bit of Scholastic web-spinning. It is a kind of necessary flourish, a bow to divinity. The statement has the air of learned finality but it is easy to see that Aristotle's terms applied in this way to God, to angels, and to the first matter have the vaguest possible content. Hidden in the Scholastic formula is the whole history of the effort to read metaphysics into Genesis. "The earth was without form and void," said the simple account. To the subtle Schoolmen with their "forms" and their creation out of nothing, the text became a bottomless abyss of theology. We shall see presently what Browne could do with it.

It is apparent from the whole that we have here a philosophy grounded on Thomas Aquinas. Browne believes in a transcendent creator who made the world in time and out of nothing as the artist fashions his materials. It is equally clear that the determining bias is the search for final causes. "This is the cause I grope after in the works of nature." But his is a search which does not stop with the mechanism. To have made the world was "but his art." He is not satisfied merely with understanding the machine. To find the laws of motion which produce eclipses is "excellent speculation," but Browne asks not only how but why. He is enticed by this "sweeter piece of reason." He never stops brooding over the ultimate question that carries him beyond the bounds of thought into the secret mind of God. No analysis into a chemical or mechanical formula will do. That is the outer portal only, the merest shadow of the truth behind. The clanging world is a word, not a system of invariable laws. The mood never changes and years later he writes *The Garden of Cyrus* to push speculation as far as he can. Things are arranged in fives, yes, but why? "Could we satisfy ourselves in the position of the lights above, or discover the wisdom of that order so invariably maintained in the fixed stars of heaven; could we have any light, why the stellary part of the first mass separated into this order, that the girdle of Orion should ever maintain its line, and the two stars in Charles' wain never leave pointing at the pole star, we might abate the Pythagorical music of the spheres, the sevenfold pipe of Pan, and the strange cryptography of Gaffarel in his starry book of heaven." [10]

In other words, he wants to push the teleological assumptions of Galen's physiology (certainly a most pious work) into his study of the great cosmic machine, and, there too, to ask not only how but why. And he blames Aristotle for stopping short of this speculation. This seems at first a very curious remark, for Aristotle was certainly a confirmed teleologist, a thinker, it might be supposed, after Browne's own heart. And when one compares them, there is

[10] *The Garden of Cyrus*, chap. iii.

apparently little to choose as to teleology between Galen's *De usu partium* and such a work as Aristotle's *De generatione animalium*. Both argue strictly from adaptation to design. Bacon saw that it was this very preoccupation that had blocked the progress of pure science. Yet on the other hand, there was in this biology of Aristotle the cloven hoof, and Browne detected it. Aristotle's creator is thwarted by his materials, his nature is an independent force; God did not make the mole's eyes with infallible adaptation to their purpose, they are congenitally arrested — a mutilated fragment. It is this hesitating instinct not only for dualism, but for the evolutionary development of nature, an instinct alive all through the Middle Ages, but destined still to wait two more centuries for full confirmation, that Browne profoundly distrusts. It is to him "an imperfect piece of philosophy." In short, his God is the infallible unthwarted workman, whose creation is without flaw, perfect in all its parts.

But to rest here would be too much like the "gross rusticity" which he despises. He turns his attention from the immensities of the solar system to what proves to be his peculiar preoccupation — the intricate mechanism of the microcosm, nature in her tiniest structure. He will not gape with ruder heads at whales, elephants, and other "prodigious pieces of nature"; he reserves his wonder for the curious mathematics of nature's "little citizens." Now this might be thought an indication of a really scientific temper, and in a way it is. When the young Socrates once rebuked Parmenides for despising dirt and hair and other small and mean things, he showed a genuine scientific spirit. Browne shows it in the same way. He seems to be a real observer, who goes beyond the medieval concern with only the broadest and roughest confirmations of a divine plan in the world. There seems also to be a kind of scientific pride in his turning from those "general pieces of wonder" which he mentions, such as the problems of the tides and of magnetism, to the "cosmography of myself." He has the air of scorning these large questions which travel and scientific excitement, he feels, had stimulated unduly. But this attitude is not so scientific as it seems. For certainly it was in the realm of astronomical mathematics that the really great achievements were being accomplished at that very moment. Browne simply represents the majority in being unaware of it. And as for psychology, interest in that was no new thing; it was a subject of feverish interest. But the fact is that it was the least fruitful science of the day. It seems to have been recognized in the higher circles that the times were not ripe for it, and there was too much danger of conflict with the church. Bacon handles it gingerly, and Sprat, as we have already seen, tells us with amusing bluntness that the Royal Society had decided to bar discussions of God and the soul until it knew more about natural philosophy; they were afraid, he says, of "falling in talking instead of working." Browne's interest in the human "compendium" is after all, old-fashioned, and this bent of his indicates not so much exactness in method as an extraordinary fascination for little things.

The study of detail must of course lead to new knowledge, and actually did in his case, but he carries into it precisely the same assumption — the teleological. Yet he loves minutiae because they show him the workman at his deftest, engaged in inconceivably delicate carving. The really interesting fact is this: that it proves impossible to fix the attention on the minutest structure of nature without, as one probes deeper, coming to realize to at least some degree that there is no stopping place, that the plant or insect organism is not static, but vital and flowing: one suspects in time the imperceptible passage from inanimate to animate. Now Browne had no real microscope and plant cells were not to be discovered in his century, but this predilection of his was to lead him into haunting half-glimpses of nature's secret. He makes no definite discoveries, but he has a different feeling for plastic nature in *The Garden of Cyrus*. Unconsciously he travels over again the very road that Aristotle took.

So here in these early pages, he is compelled to track the footprints of nature not in the simple biblical way, but, like all the Middle Ages, in the Greek way. It was a half-conscious influence. *Natura nihil agit frustra,* he says, thinking it a cap to his theology. But this "only indisputable axiom" is a pitfall, for, metaphor though it may be, it carries with it the whole Greek conception of nature as an independent force, as the universal mother, as the "prudent housewife." And the next sentence is still more unescapably in the same direction. "In the most imperfect creatures, and such as were not preserved in the ark, but, having their seeds and principles in the womb of nature, are everywhere,

where the power of the sun is, in these is the wisdom of his hand discovered." The story of Noah's ark did not account for bees and spiders and gnats and myriads of still smaller forms of life, and in their bewilderment the Middle Ages reluctantly fell back on the theory of spontaneous generation. It was nothing more nor less than hylozoism. Browne accepts it as a commonplace of science and refers to it repeatedly in various parts of his works. Harvey's famous principle of *omne vivum ex ovo* was not given to the world until 1651, and Harvey himself had to leave the proof of it to the future. There are indications in *The Garden of Cyrus* that Browne was acquainted with the principle, but he evidently clung to the older belief in spontaneous generation to the last.

So far, then, we have simply the Scholastic natural philosophy couched in the usual terms and betraying the usual inconsistencies. The one fresh and perhaps promising feature is Browne's fondness for nature's miniatures.

We come to section 16, the heart of the discussion—a beautiful and justly famous passage. It begins with a magnificent sentence. "Thus there are two books from whence I collect my divinity; besides that written one of God, another of his servant nature, that universal and public manuscript, that lies expansed unto the eyes of all." This strikes a different note. To be sure, there is nothing in it that a Church Father might not have said, but there is a spirit in that fine phrase "the universal and public manuscript," and in the appreciation of Greek religion and the rebuke to Christians "who cast a more careless eye on these common hieroglyphics, and disdain to suck divinity from the flowers of nature," which outstrips theology in the breadth of its poetic sympathy with natural religion. None of the new generation who had this expansive attitude toward nature were much afraid of atheism. It is in this spirit that Browne goes on to find what verbal formula he can for his conception of nature. He refuses naturalism: "nor do I so forget God as to adore the name of nature"; he refuses that bare Aristotelian definition, "the principle of motion and rest" which scholasticism had bandied back and forth for fruitless centuries as the sum of its feeble physics. He has no interest in that. He needs only a symbol, but he wants one that will come nearest to expressing his conviction that nature is the union between creator and created. The term he chooses is a striking and a puzzling one. Nature, he says, is "that straight and regular line, that settled and constant course the wisdom of God hath ordained the actions of his creatures, according to their several kinds." Now the question is, what does Browne mean by this word "line"? Clearly from the standpoint of science he means nothing whatever. And yet as a symbol the word deserves a little attention, for it is broadly indicative of a point of view; it suggests his attitude, as far as he reveals it, toward the question of dualism.

It is in this connection, though we certainly çannot push it far, that our interest is aroused in certain terms and modes of thought of the Cabbala. The Cabbalists explained the paradox of infinity creating a finite world, or of individuation out of the absolute, by a peculiarly mystical doctrine which they referred to as the "contraction," whereby the infinite limits himself in order to leave an empty space in the world. Totality had to become manifold in order to appear and become visible in definite things, and this power, which runs through the universe and gives it form and being, they called the "line." The first cause, they said, retired into its own nature, limited and concealed itself, in order that the phenomenon might become possible.[11] It is not possible to draw any strong inferences from Browne's use of the term "line," but it is interesting to find Culverwel, in a passage already quoted, using the same term a little later in the early days of the Platonist movement. "Nature," he says, "is that regular line which the wisdom of God himself has drawn in being"; and he proceeds, "it is a principle of working in spirituals as well as *principium motus et quietis*," it is in fact "Being itself." Perhaps Christian and Jew alike took this word from current allegories on the verse "Their line is gone out through all the earth." [12] It may have been a common symbol. At any rate,

[11] See the article on the "Cabbala" by Louis Ginsberg in the *Jewish Encyclopedia*.
[12] I have been able to find some confirmation of this in the *Zohar* (English translation, 5 vols., London: the Soncino Press, 1934). It contains many commentaries on the nineteenth psalm. There is space here for two short illustrations: "As for those words of wisdom, 'their line is gone out through all the earth,' they trace the measure and the plan of all celestial and all terrestrial habitations; it is indeed through those words that the heavens

it has the sound of a technical term, and Browne is sufficiently fond of it to use it twice. In his rough verses in section 13 he exhorts the scientific inquirer to

> Rally the scattered causes; and that line,
> Which nature twists, be able to untwine.

It seemed to satisfy him and others as the best symbol for the unity of that great order which embraces both the spiritual and the material, and which admits no dualism anywhere.

But this is very vaguely worked out. We get no satisfactory explanation of the "line" of nature. "To make a revolution every day," he continues, "is the nature of the sun, because of that necessary course which God hath ordained it." He seems to think of nature as embodied law, self-moving for the most part, and a kind of aspect of God's character and power. And yet clearly God is separate from the process, and natural law is not the invariable behavior which modern science assumes, but subject to supernatural interruption. Browne assigns a ready reason for this: God sometimes steps into the process "lest the arrogancy of our reason should question his power and conclude he could not." Measured alongside the Platonists, this is very naive. And Browne is not troubled by that consciousness of the slowness and mistakes in the organic world which drove these men to believe that nature is a stupid and recalictrant power. As to why nature's processes are so roundabout, Browne thinks that God prefers to work in that way, "like an excellent artist," or "a skillful geometrician"; instead of making a new creation He prefers to economize his materials; instead of a freehand stroke, He prefers the compass and ruler. "And thus," Browne says as a kind of summary, "I call the effects of nature the works of God, whose hand and instrument she only is." In other words, God is a transcendent artist who has made a vital mechanism which he controls for the most part from the outside by the laws he has imposed upon it, though occasionally he arbitrarily invades them. Such a view

were made, and it is through the praises sung in those words that the earth was made" (I, 36). And another commentary on the same psalm: "Now the Tree of Life extends from above downward, and it is the Sun which illumines all. Its radiance commences at the top and extends through the whole trunk in a straight line" (V, 203). See also III, 392 and 358. In the *Zohar* the term "line" is associated with various mystical emanation theories, but I have not been able to identify any doctrine of "contraction" (or "retraction") there.

is simply and straightforwardly orthodox; it shows no concern about the problems of dualism.

In the next sentence, however, there is a new turn. The whole creation, he declares, is beautiful, without any ugliness or deformity in any of its parts, and the least pleasing organisms have the beauty of structural perfection and adaptation. This is a point of affinity with the teaching of Thomas Aquinas that "every creature exists for the perfection of the entire universe," [13] or with the feeling of the Stoics for the harmony of nature in all its parts. "Corporeal creatures," says St. Thomas, "according to their nature are good, though this good is not universal, but partial and limited . . . though each quality is good in itself. . . . The same thing may be evil in some respects, but good in others. And this could not be, if bodies were essentially evil and harmful." [14] And Marcus Aurelius could enjoy seeing the gaping jaws of wild beasts in the arena, and ignore the bloodshed which he abhorred, for, he writes, "Many things though if looked at apart from their settings . . . are far from being comely, yet as resultants from the operations of nature have an added charm and excite our admiration. And so, if a man has sensibility and a deeper insight into the workings of the universe, scarcely anything . . . but will seem to him to form in its own peculiar way a pleasing adjunct to the whole." [15] When Browne says that he "cannot tell by what logic we call a toad, a bear, or an elephant ugly" he is parting company with the ugly dualism of the day. And it is a moral and esthetic rather than a scientific revolt. It involves the scientist's appreciation of structural adaptation, but it involves far more the temperament of the inveterate moral philosopher, who thinks primarily in terms of intrinsic beauty and moral sanctions. When Hobbes said there was nothing in itself either beautiful or ugly, he jarred upon the Cambridge

[13] *Summa Theologica*, I, Q. 65, art. 2. (Translation of the Fathers of the English Dominican Province.)

[14] *Ibid.*, art. 1. On the contrary, St. Augustine said, "I confess I am ignorant why mice and frogs were created, or flies and worms. . . . All creatures are either useful, hurtful, or superfluous to us. . . . As for the hurtful creatures, we are either punished, or disciplined, or terrified by them, so that we may not cherish and love this life." (Quoted in Andrew D. White, *A History of the Warfare of Science with Theology in Christendom* (New York, 1903), I, 30.

[15] *Meditations*, trans. C. R. Haines (Loeb Classical Library), III, 2.

Platonists in the same way that he would have jarred upon Browne. It was a view of esthetics that they could not admit. All that God made was good, Browne insists, and "conformable to his will, which abhors deformity and is the rule of order and beauty."

This dislike of dualism touches the center of the problem. Obviously Browne is too close to the scriptural view, too Hebraic, to go far with the Cabbalists or the Platonists, but he strongly shares their feeling for unity in the world. He is able to share this feeling without wrestling very strenuously with any of the problems involved in his theology. We may take *Paradise Lost* as the supreme illustration of the difficulties that spring out of that theology when a mind like Milton's tries to elaborate it and to mold into a unity all the disparate philosophical and scientific components that centuries of thought have evolved. He does it with wonderful artistic energy, notwithstanding the added drawback of the narrative and scenical framework. But his treatment of the origin of evil is doomed to failure, the revolt of Satan only carries it back a step, and when he comes to deal with nature and creation, he parts company altogether with the orthodox doctrine that the world was created out of nothing. Milton believes that matter is part of the eternal being of God, and he distinguishes between chaos (primeval, unorganized matter), which is evil and hostile to God, and nature (organized matter, created in time out of chaos), which is good. His explanation of the creation of the world out of chaos is more or less in biblical terms; his conception of chaos itself is Neo-Platonic or Cabbalistic.

In the second book, when the gates of hell are opened for Satan,

> Before their eyes in sudden view appear
> The secrets of the hoary deep, a dark
> Illimitable ocean without bound,
> Without dimension, where length, breadth, and highth
> And time and place are lost; where eldest Night
> And Chaos, ancestors of Nature, hold
> Eternal anarchy, amidst the noise
> Of endless wars, and by confusion stand.
> For hot, cold, moist, and dry, four champions fierce

> Strive here for maistrie, and to battle bring
> Their embryon atoms. . . .
>   Into this wild abyss
> The womb of Nature and perhaps her grave,

Satan plunges, and makes his dark and perilous journey to the top of the new world. At last from that station

>   the sacred influence
> Of light appears, and from the walls of Heav'n
> Shoots far into the bosom of dim Night
> A glimmering dawn; here Nature first begins
> Her fardest verge, and Chaos to retire
> As from her outmost works a broken foe.

A discussion of Milton's views of matter and nature would lead far afield. Obviously, however, they involve great difficulties.[16] Sir Thomas Browne, not having to labor under Milton's artistic handicap, avoids this crucial difficulty by simply pushing a paradox to the edge of absurdity — or sublimity, according as his reader may decide. "There is no deformity but in monstrosity; wherein, notwithstanding, there is a kind of beauty. . . . To speak yet more narrowly, there was never anything ugly or misshapen, but the chaos: wherein, notwithstanding, to speak strictly, there was no deformity, because no form." The plain man of the street may well protest that this progressive strictness of speech carries us well beyond the bounds of intelligible language. We will not stop to point out how repellent Browne's esthetics would be to the Calvinists, with their sense of sin, of the curse that rests on creation, and of the separation of heaven and hell. The point is that Browne buoyantly avoids the difficulties that troubled his contemporaries. He does not deny the reality of the finite world with the idealists, he does not limit God's power in any way as the Neo-Platonists and Milton really did; he simply waves aside the chaos with one of those turns of language which darken rather than enlighten the understanding,

[16] Denis Saurat, *op. cit.*, pp. 231 ff., traces some of Milton's central ideas to the *Zohar*, particularly the doctrine of the "retraction." Saurat considers Milton a kind of monistic pantheist, who found confirmation of his ideas in the Cabbala and took from it as much as could be assimilated to Western modes of thought.

and takes refuge in esthetics. That is his method of saving the day for his perfect God and perfect world. So, in that fascinating way of his, he eats his cake and has it too.

And then he brings the passage to a climax with that famous series of epigrams to which we have been leading. "Now nature is not at variance with art, nor art with nature; they being both the servants of his providence. Art is the perfection of nature. Were the world as it was the sixth day, there were yet a chaos. Nature hath made one world, and art another. In brief, all things are artificial: for nature is the art of God." Browne is of course presenting in this fine passage the old opposition between daedal nature, conceived as a vital force, cunning, subtle, inevitable in her operations, and conscious art, the power of intelligent invention and design which man first perceives in himself, and then transfers to his idea of God. It presents two entirely different worlds, the state of nature, and the state of arts, sciences, and organized society. The one is instinctive, "natural," a part of the organic function, the other is external, deliberately invented, fashioned out of the given material. The one accounts for native, uncultivated growth, for barbarous states of society, the other for intelligent and conscious refinements and adaptations and developments.

With his accustomed prodigal ease, Shakespeare packs all the philosophy of Browne's epigram, "Art is the perfection of nature," into a few lines of poetry. When Perdita says she will have no gilliflowers in her garden, because she has heard it said

> There is an art which in their piedness shares
> With great creating nature,

Polixenes answers,
> Say there be;
> Yet nature is made better by no mean
> But nature makes that mean; so, over that art
> Which you say adds to nature, is an art
> That nature makes. You see, sweet maid, we marry
> A gentle scion to the wildest stock,
> And make conceive a bark of baser kind
> By bud of nobler race. This is an art

THE ART OF GOD

> Which does mend nature, change it rather, but
> The art itself is Nature.[17]

Nature is the creator, and all that art can do is to direct her. Yet after all Browne has it differently. He never shares Shakespeare's or Spenser's feeling for daedal nature, the creative mother. Nature herself is not an artist; she is not another name for God, far less a coeval principle with Him. "All things are artificial," he insists in the last analysis. There is but one artist, and he is always apart from his work. In short, Browne does not find God in nature in the pantheistic fashion of nineteenth-century poetry; he does not commune with the Presence in the round earth and the living air. Yet if we must find a philosophic tag for his beautiful saying that "Nature is the art of God," the nearest word is immanence.

III

But all this must be joined with the two following sections, for Browne now broadens his thought to include the inevitable next topic — "fortune." Nature, art, and chance — this is the historic triumvirate of causes. The words are mere shorthand for the three philosophies that were mentioned at the beginning of this chapter — the chance arrangement of atoms, the creative power of nature, and external, intelligent design. Browne is walking here in a well-beaten path that leads us back through the Middle Ages at least to Plato. In the *Laws* Plato devotes the tenth book to a discussion of this ancient threefold opposition, and he combats the atheism that arose in the state when men thought that the fundamental principles were chance and nature, and that art was later and of mortal birth.

"They say that the greatest and fairest things are the work of nature and of chance, the lesser of art, which, receiving from nature the greater and primeval creations, molds and fashions all those lesser works which are generally termed artificial. . . . They say that . . . Art sprang up afterwards and out of these, mortal and of mortal birth, and produced in play certain images and very partial imitations of the truth. . . . And they say that politics cooperate with nature, but in a less degree, and have

[17] *The Winter's Tale*, IV. iv. 87 ff.

more of art; also that legislation is entirely a work of art, and is based on assumptions which are not true. . . . These people would say that the Gods exist not by nature, but by art, and by the laws of states, which are different in different places, according to the agreement of those who make them . . . and that the principles of justice have no existence at all in nature. . . ."[18]

Plato goes on to prove, with arduous wrestling, the priority of mind by his doctrine of the self-moved, and so to establish the fact that there are gods, that they have a care for man, and that they are inflexible in justice. The whole discussion offers a striking comparison with Milton's eternally transcendent God, reduced none the less to carving his kingdom out of the primordial domains of hot, cold, moist, and dry. But Plato's classic discussion serves as well as any to bring out further aspects of the matter. A few years after Browne had said that nature is the art of God, Hobbes used the same words and then proceeded to build up a ruthlessly mechanical and naturalistic psychology and political economy which Plato would have considered a rejuvenation of the atheism that he hated. The Cambridge Platonists recognized it for what it was, and pitted against it their belief that reason and morality are real and primal in the universe. If man is only a congeries of appetites and passions, said Cudworth, he sinks back into nature, and there is "not the slightest shadow of argument to prove a deity by." In this matter of nature, art, and chance, the one thing that these men insisted on was moral freedom and responsibility, and they denied every kind of fatalism or external control.

Browne's conception of "fate" and "fortune," on the other hand, is a good deal colored by certain personal predilections, that have the tinge, most of us would say, of popular superstitions. The Church, no less than the classical philosophers, had deprecated the popular meaning of the word "fate." [19] But the average Christian had clung to that fear of the influence of stars,

[18] Jowett's translation.
[19] Thomas Aquinas says, "The ordering of human actions, the principle of which is the will, must be ascribed to God alone. So therefore in as much as all that happens here below is subject to Divine Providence, as being pre-ordained, and as it were fore-spoken, we can admit the existence of fate: although the holy doctors avoided the use of this word, on account

the malignity of spirits, and the blighting effect of bad luck which sent men as often to astrologers and weavers of spells as to church. They were fatalists by temperament and training, and their theory of life was well represented by the wheel of fortune; to rise and fall was the mysterious law of human life. "Fortune" meant the unalterable destiny that the stars held, under the control of divine Providence. The Renaissance, however, had its effect on the notion of "fortune." Probably the atheism that lurked in the word began to inspire different emotions. Men were less cringing; they often developed the impudent defiance of the Greek satirists. There is, for instance, Bacon's essay "Of Fortune." From the point of view of the courtier, he says, fortune is to be diplomatically reckoned with. It is true that for the most part events are explainable; a man can separate the elements of success as he can distinguish small stars — "the way of fortune is like the milken way in the sky." Yet, it must be admitted, "certainly there be, whose fortunes are like Homer's verses, that have a slide and easiness more than the verses of other poets." They have the silver spoon. So it is with all success. But it is not politic to admit it, either to man or God. "All wise men, to decline the envy of their own virtues, use to ascribe them to Providence and Fortune; for so they may the better assume them; and, besides, it is greatness in a man to be the care of the higher powers." This seems like the graceful sweep of the courtier's cap towards God.

Browne is utterly different. Here for the first time there creeps in something of his peculiarly somber and morbid cast of thought. To begin with, Providence in human life for him is quite a different thing from Providence in nature. His moral world is full of satanic and angelic influences. Furthermore, God's ways with men are dark and winding, and he works against nature to cut off our days. A great deal of this feeling is temperamental. Much of *Religio Medici* is overshadowed by the conviction that there is a "secret glome [thread] or bottom of our days." [20] One feels that Browne was not stimulated but depressed

of those who twisted its application to a certain force in the position of the stars. Hence Augustine says (*De Civ. Dei*, V, 1): If anyone ascribes human affairs to fate, meaning thereby the will or power of God, let him keep to his opinion, but hold his tongue." *Summa Theologica*, I, Q. 116, art. 2.

[20] *Religio Medici*, I, 43.

by "the perpetual and waking providence that fulfills and accomplisheth them." He was superstitious, and, as he confesses, he had a "piece of the leaden planet" in him. He had brooded much on the average span of mortality: "Let them not therefore complain of immaturity that die about thirty: they fall but like the whole world." [21] He had brooded too on the reason why men should die so often on their birthdays — "that the tail of the snake should return into its mouth precisely at that time." It was to be his own fate by an almost uncanny coincidence. And he is driven to conclude, with a good deal of intensity, that "there is therefore some other hand that twines the thread of life than that of nature: we are not only ignorant in antipathies and occult qualities; our ends are as obscure as our beginnings; the line of our days is drawn by night, and the various effects therein by a pencil that is invisible; wherein, though we confess our ignorance, I am sure we do not err if we say it is the hand of God." [22]

It is not surprising then that his ideas about fortune are what they prove to be — somber and quaintly illogical. He deserts the high ground of God's comparatively regular operation in nature for "another way, full of meanders and labyrinths, whereof the devil and spirits have no exact ephemerides: and that is a more particular and obscure method of his providence; directing the operations of individuals and single essences: this we call fortune, that serpentine and crooked line, whereby he draws those actions his wisdom intends, in a more unknown and secret way." [23] He thinks then, as most people still do, that human events are subject to a special providential economy. Here God is still the active and direct cause of every circumstance. Browne sees and wonders at the evidence of this in his own life and in world history; and his aim is to retain faith not only in personal Providence but in the occult sciences as well, bringing the whole, with medieval inclusiveness, into the grand chain of causation. The effort is a quaint one, and yet he manages to raise it to majestic levels. "Those that hold, that all things are governed by fortune, had not erred, had they not persisted there." [24] There are quiet but

[21] *Ibid.*
[22] *Ibid.*
[23] *Ibid.*, I, 17.
[24] *Ibid.*, I, 18.

memorable sentences like this one that have the ring of Greek poetry.

But he has difficulties on his hands, and some humorously of his own making.[25] The victory of '88 was not fortune but a stroke of Providence. What then, says the skeptic, had God to do with the victory of the Dutch against Spain, a circumstance singularly lacking in any evidence of divine interposition? But Sir Thomas is not discomfited. This victory, he says, "I cannot altogether ascribe to the ingenuity and industry of the people, but the mercy of God, that hath disposed them to such a thriving genius." For him history is indeed a quaintly crooked line. "All cannot be happy at once; for, because the glory of one state depends upon the ruin of another, there is a revolution and vicissitude of their greatness, and must obey the swing of that wheel, not moved by intelligences, but by the hand of God, whereby all estates arise to their zenith and vertical points, according to their predestinated periods." The story of mankind is not a march of moral forces or of economic determinism, but a predestined cycle outside human control.

There is, too, a delightfully illogical proof of the logic of praying before casting lots. Since the lie of the dice is predetermined it is proper to pray for the winning number! And there is another difficulty — the notorious luck of fools and of the wicked which has earned fortune the uncomplimentary soubriquets of whore, bawd, and strumpet. This matter Browne handles more reverently than Bacon does, and with a sterner ethics than the orthodox religious argument about future compensations in heaven and hell. He answers it out of the bitter and enduring wisdom of the old Stoics, Seneca and Epictetus, contemning outward misfortune, had said that the wise man alone is a true part of the universe, the rich are the real outcasts. Browne outdoes them. With what seems like a burst of bravado he cries, "Let Providence provide for fools . . . those that are able of body and mind he leaves to their deserts; to those of weaker merits, he imparts a larger portion."

Again there is the difficulty of astrology. How reconcile Providence with lucky stars? But Browne answers — and his argument

[25] *Ibid.*, I, 17.

is of course as valid as any answer that the religious determinist makes to such questions — that "if to be born under Mercury disposeth us to be witty, under Jupiter to be wealthy; I do not owe a knee unto these, but unto that merciful hand that hath ordered my indifferent and uncertain nativity unto such benevolous aspects."

In short, he denies that there are any evidences of chance in human history. Fortune is a "careless term" for divine Providence, which works through universal and reliable causes. "There is no liberty for causes to operate in a loose and straggling way." And yet the point is that he cannot help thinking of the line of causation in human affairs as, if not loose and straggling, at least serpentine. The distinction between these two aspects of Providence has always been a natural one: man is too complex, too conscious now of free will, now of impotence, too strongly convinced of his importance, for it to be otherwise, and he tends to distinguish between the straight line of nature and the crooked line of human destiny.

And now he links together all he had said about these first and second causes with one of those sweeping perorations of his. With the roll of the phrase "All things begin and end in the Almighty," it marches on to the end.[26] It is true that the march is nothing less than jaunty. Bacon had given his grave and coldly orthodox opinion that "out of the contemplation of nature, or ground of human knowledges to induce any verity or persuasion concerning the points of faith, is in my judgment not safe. . . . For the heathen themselves conclude as much in that excellent and divine fable of the golden chain: *That men and gods were not able to draw Jupiter down to the earth; but contrariwise Jupiter was able to draw them up to heaven.* So as we ought not to attempt to draw down or to submit the mysteries of God to our reason; but contrariwise to raise and advance our reason to the divine truth."[27] But Browne is the troubadour, and he dismisses Homer's chain with the same buoyancy that had made him delight in Tertullian. "There is a nearer way to heaven than Homer's chain; an easy logic may conjoin heaven and earth in one argument, and with less than a sorites, resolve all things

[26] *Ibid.*, I, 18.   [27] *Advancement of Learning*, II, vi, 1.

into God." And then in a final sentence, almost pantheistic in its inclusiveness, he disposes of the whole matter of causation. "For though we christen effects by their most sensible and nearest causes, yet is God the true and infallible cause of all; whose concourse, though it be general, yet doth it subdivide itself into the particular actions of every thing, and is that spirit, by which each singular essence not only subsists, but performs its operation."

What is to be said of all this? Certainly with the cadence of this sentence in one's ears, it will at least be said that such words as transcendence and immanence and pantheism are bloodless formulas for religious passion like Browne's. Whichever of these may best describe him, he belongs to the age of faith. The structure of his thought is like the first Gothic cathedrals — built for love, not for a creed. But it has structure; it is not a rhapsody or an improvization. These five sections are a kind of choral prelude to what is to follow, and the persistent organ point upon which all the solemn music is built up is of course teleology. To what extent the divine artist is conceived as outside his work, to what extent as immanent in it is not so easy to decide. In successive phases of thought we have first, "a block world without a career," in William James' phrase, ended already in the mind of God, a mere point of time, thought into being by the blast of his mouth; then a manufactured product, deliberately and laboriously wrought by the artist through cycles of time, and constantly elaborated by his fingers; then a plastic nature to which the creator gives laws and in which he is indwelling as immanent energy. What this "art of God," this *natura daedala rerum* is, and where the dividing line, where the point of intersection between creator and created, Browne as yet does not attempt to say. But in the face of nature he sees primarily beauty, order, and ultimate unity, and the argument from creation to creator seems to him self-evident. He would have agreed with Kant that the starry heavens and the moral law are the two awe-inspiring things. The problems of teleology never presented themselves to him as they did to more solid thinkers like Bacon or Cudworth. He did not feel any ineluctable opposition in the immemorial concepts of nature, fate, and God.

It remained perhaps for Kant to state the opposition clearly and to put these concepts into something like a final relation to each other. He saw the crux of the difficulty, as Bacon had: how to get a God who cares for each creature into a world of nature, a world, that is, of unalterable law. Special Providence is a contradiction in terms: "it is to let him who is himself the entire cause of the changes in the universe make good any shortcomings in his own predetermining Providence (which to require this must be defective) in the course of this world." [28] The terms nature, fate, and God must then belong to different spheres of thought. All that happens in the phenomenal world is due to the operation of nature, by unalterable laws which we may call fate, and the term "nature" rather than "Providence" is the proper one for us in view of our limited human reason, but the laws of nature show design so clearly that from the religious and transcendental point of view they are to be regarded as the deep wisdom of a higher though inscrutable cause working toward the realization of the final purpose of the human race and the world. The author of *Religio Medici* never really faces the dilemma of which modern philosophy is so conscious. He belongs to a world where miracle was almost the rule rather than the exception, and where as in a family or petty state, the cosmic economy was directly and immediately administered by Providence in person.

IV

But this is only the beginning of Browne's speculations. "The art of God" proves to be his primary and lifelong quest, and in later parts of *Religio Medici* and in *Vulgar Errors* and *The Garden of Cyrus* he studies it from many and fascinatingly different angles. We must try to follow the scent through some of these turns of thought. In *Religio Medici*[29] he returns to the macrocosm again by way of some remarks on witches and guardian angels, which, in turn, suggests to him the subject of the world spirit. This is the notion which the Cambridge Platonists were soon to reintroduce into theology. In the Middle Ages it was impossible to account for life except on the assumption of "soul,"

---

[28] Kant, "Eternal Peace."
[29] I, 32.

and Browne simply inherits hazy opinions that ranged all the way from belief in an *anima mundi* to Descartes' denial of psychic powers to everything but man. The common opinion was that each order of creation had its separate kind of "soul," continuous in the species, but mortal in the individual, man alone having the higher or "rational" immortal soul. Browne, with his usual catholic willingness, seems ready to entertain the unorthodox notion of an *anima mundi*, a universal spirit of nature. At least he is noncommittal about it. "Now, besides these particular and divided spirits," he says, "there may be (for aught I know) a universal and common spirit to the whole world. It was the opinion of Plato, and it is yet of the hermetical philosophers." He thinks, vaguely enough, that if each species has its common "nature," there may be a general and inclusive world-nature.

The argument illustrates how very loosely he uses the word nature. But the point to notice is that he thinks of this doubtful *anima mundi* not in the terms of Plato, but of the alchemists. For whatever be the truth about the world soul, he goes on, "I am sure there is a common spirit, that plays within us, yet makes no part of us; and that is the spirit of God; the fire and scintillation of that noble and mighty essence, which is the life and radical heat of spirits, and those essences that know not the virtue of the sun; a fire quite contrary to the fire of hell." These words are suggestive enough of alchemical processes and terms, but the next sentence is conclusive. "This is that gentle heat that brooded on the waters, and in six days hatched the world; this is that irradiation that dispels the mists of hell . . . and preserves the region of the mind in serenity. Whosoever feels not the warm gale and gentle ventilation of this spirit, though I feel his pulse, I dare not say he lives; for truly, without this, to me there is no heat under the tropic; nor any light, though I dwelt in the body of the sun." "Gentle heat" (or, as they called it, *incendium amoris*), "hatch," "warm gale," "gentle ventilation" are among the most familiar words of the fraternity. Browne adopts them with striking imaginative effect. He has turned the first verses of Genesis into Hermetic symbolism, and conceived the world process as a great alchemist furnace. Here is suggested, too, the occult notion of the cosmic levels — the serene region of the mind, the mystical state of the Christian, without whose spiritual pulse and heat there is no life. Yet he guards carefully against pantheism, as always; this common spirit "plays within us, yet makes no part of us." The passage serves to show how facile and striking is his borrowing of imagery, and how artistically restrained. Compared with the meaningless extravagance of a thorough-paced alchemist like Ashmole, for example, the idea is kept thoroughly in hand. But at the same time, the play of thought and images seems to have a certain new intensity. Browne seldom if ever shows any degree of religious rapture, but there is a subdued glow in such a phrase as "the fire and scintillation of that noble and mighty essence, which is the life and radical heat of spirits"; it is in a different key from the "art of God" passage. It is couched in terms that more clearly express the feeling for immanence — for vital generative force, and brooding power.

Perhaps we cannot follow the trail any further just here, but the subject is immediately reintroduced from a slightly different standpoint. It is in the course of a subtly delicate fantasy on the nature of spirits in the following section.[30] The passage beginning here is probably the most subtle thing in *Religio Medici*. Here more than anywhere else in the book our young physician is at once the delicate Ariel of metaphysics and the spirit who questions. There is something of a thirst after forbidden knowledge in it that may have conjured up for some readers the names of Faustus or Bruno. It flies into regions which were still a little terrorizing to the orthodox, at least enough so to earn Browne the name of atheist. He kindles at notions here that carry him far afield of the earlier symbolism of the daedal finger of God. What, he asks, is the nature of spirits? "Now, if you demand my opinion and metaphysics of their natures, I confess them very shallow, most of them in a negative way, like that of God" — God, that is, is absolute and unknowable, of whom nothing can be predicated — "or in a comparative, between ourselves and fellow creatures: for there is in this universe a stair or manifest scale, of creatures, rising not disorderly, or in confusion, but with a comely method and proportion." This is the scale of life, in-

[30] I, 33.

volving five steps from the inanimate to the angelic, the highest having to perfection all the intellectual faculties that are rudimentary in man. This was the orthodox psychology, about which more will be said presently. But the ladder of creation is too simple an idea for Browne. He has the philosopher's unquenchable thirst for unity, and it is first clearly apparent at this point. Just where is the crossing point, the decussation, of mind and matter? That is the question.

The first answer is one common to both Jewish and Christian mysticism and drawn out of the Genesis allegories: namely, the metaphysics of light. "I cannot with those in that great Father,[31] securely interpret the work of the first day, *Fiat lux,* to the creation of angels; though I confess there is not any creature that hath so near a glimpse of their nature as light in the sun and elements; we style it a bare accident; but, where it subsists alone, 'tis a spiritual substance, and may be an angel: in brief, conceive light invisible, and that is a spirit." Browne advances this notion with hesitation. It is certainly mystic enough. But it is a mystical region familiar to readers of patristic commentaries on *Genesis,* traversed over and over again by those fathers whose imagination was fired by the opening fiat of creation, "Let there be light." From Philo to Bruno or Robert Fludd there is an elaborate literature discussing from every possible point of view the secrets that are hidden in light if man knew its nature. *Lux est umbra Dei* is perhaps more than a symbol for Browne, and he is entering a path of speculation that he will follow much further later on.

One should not explore conceptions like these too rigorously. To say with Browne that "light is a spiritual substance and may be an angel," that beneath its material accident, namely brightness, is an invisible or spiritual brightness, is to climb too far into the sun of mystical ideas, where the word becomes the thing. Light is still a mystery, but in the days when it had scarcely been brought into the domain of physics, when Digby could report in his treatise on the *Nature of Bodies* that a friend had collected sunbeams through glasses in the form of a purplish powder, to

---

[31] Either St. Chrysostom (*Homilies*) or St. Augustine (*City of God*). (Keck's note.)

the amount of two ounces a day, the passage between the physics and metaphysics of light was easy enough to yield almost any results. And yet, judging from the recent vocabulary of physics, the present theories of light seem mystical enough to be almost hospitable again to Browne's angels. But whatever we may say of the physics, the poetry is clear. Nature is alive with life in the aether, and its splendor and shimmer is God. Here, as the least corporeal thing in nature, is a point of union.

But it is difficut indeed to pursue such an idea without going completely over to pantheism. And Browne is carried to the very edge of it. For if angels live in light, in fact *are* spiritual and invisible light, what becomes of heaven, or any spiritual *place* whatever? Browne makes the only logical answer. "Now for that immaterial world, methinks we need not wander so far as beyond the first movable: for even in this material fabric, the spirits walk as freely exempt from the affection of time, place, and motion, as beyond the extremest circumference. Do but extract from the corpulency of bodies, or resolve things beyond their first matter, and you discover the habitation of angels, which if I call the ubiquitary and omnipresent essence of God, I hope I shall not offend divinity: for before the creation of the world, God was really all things. For the angels he created no new world, or determinate mansion, and therefore they are everywhere where is his essence, and do live at a distance even in himself."[32] This is very beautiful; as beautiful as "Lift the stone and thou shalt find me, cleave the wood, and there am I," or as Thompson's

> Turn but a stone and start a wing.

Nevertheless, Browne certainly did offend divinity. To be sure, he says guardedly that "before the creation of the world God was really all things," and he is careful to make it clear that he believes in a "determinate mansion" for man. He safeguards, too, the transcendence of God by the orthodox argument that the infinite created a finite world and its inhabitants to satisfy the attribute of honor that needed an honorer. And to explain an *ex nihilo* world, "which much troubled the pen of the ancient philosophers," he falls back obediently on Genesis: "But Moses

[32] I, 35.

decided that question, and all is salved with the new term of a creation, that is, a production of something out of nothing." We have already asked both Milton and Browne the persistent question, What is this nothing? But this time Browne takes it out of our mouth. "And what is that? Whatsoever is opposite to something; or more exactly, that which is truly contrary unto God: for he only is. . . . God, being all things is contrary unto nothing, out of which were made all things, and so nothing became something, and omneity informed nullity into an essence." As a scholastic metaphysician, he may plume himself on these lines. He has retired into gross darkness, whither we shall not attempt to follow him. But he unquestionably gave offense in some quarters. In fact, a theologian pounced upon this very passage, accusing Browne of skirting the edge of atheism.[33]

We may note in passing another interesting fact about this passage on the habitation of angels: that Browne again falls back on alchemical terms. Ashmole says[34] that the alchemist can so handle "the universal and all-piercing spirit" that God infused into the primal chaos "as to take it from corporiety, free it from captivity, and let it loose that it may freely work as it doth in the aethereal bodies." The vocabulary and mode of thought are practically identical with Browne's.[35]

This notion of angels lurking beneath corporiety and living everywhere in God, with its taint of pantheism, is, however, scarcely the head and front of Browne's offending. He attacks the problem of nature from still another angle, the phenomenon of man. Browne's psychology will need fuller discussion later on, but certain features of it are particularly interesting at this point. What is man? For Browne the most natural definition is that man is the microcosm, the creature who duplicates in his small sphere the whole range of elements in the universe from lowest to highest, and thus contains the whole in the part. The angels, he tells us, "are certainly the magisterial and masterpieces of the creator; the flower, or as we may say, the best part of nothing" — a paradox not often quoted, but as good as anything in Browne for

[33] Sawrin's *Discourses*; cited by Wilkin, II, 375.
[34] *Theatrum Chemicum* (1652), p. 447.
[35] Cf. "Do but extract from the corpulency of bodies, etc." (I, 35).

reach of fancy and quaintness of combination. Just below the angels is man, the "amphibium," the only inhabitant of two worlds, the link between body and spirit. Without denying the theory of special creation, Browne is much impressed with the fact that man in his life plays many parts, passing from rude, inchoate embryo through the stages of vegetable, animal, human, and spiritual life. Browne is not of course thinking in evolutionary terms; the quaint word "amphibium" proves that. Man is not so much a part of the life stream as a static link in a fixed world, and he is set apart; he alone lives in divided worlds.

Browne is extremely fond of exploring the metaphysical possibilities involved in the microcosm. He had come to regard the word as more than "a pleasant trope of rhetoric," and he pursues the idea as far as he can in his restless effort to find the pulse of the machine. He feels that personality or "soul" is the very genius of the cosmos, as of its small "compendium" man, that life (to adopt a modern definition) is "the meeting place of various stages of reality." What are the component elements that one finds fused together with such infinite subtlety in the great and the small world alike? How separate them? Where are the points of intersection? Dissection has told him nothing; he has not been able to find any seat for the soul. But that does not trouble him. He knows it is there. The great problem is, how are mind and matter physically two but organically one? If one could answer that, one would understand the "art of God."

Browne does not put the question in these terms, but essentially this is what he keeps reflecting on, and he approaches it in new ways in one book after another. At this point, where he is following the clue of the microcosm, he drifts farther and farther in the direction of a kind of Platonic mysticism. The soul is hidden, he believes, beneath the accidents of the body, like potential gold in the alchemist's metal: "The smattering I have of the philosopher's stone (which is something more than the perfect exaltation of gold) hath taught me a great deal of divinity, and instructed my belief, how that immortal spirit and incorruptible substance of my soul may lie obscure, and sleep awhile within this house of flesh." [36] Again, the body turns into soul as the chrysalis

[36] I, 39.

THE ART OF GOD

into the butterfly.[37] Not only does body pass into soul in some such ways as these, so that the one is a kind of "form" of the other, but matter itself has a "form," a reality behind its accidents, which is indestructible. At the resurrection the personality will be individualized not only by the soul but by the form of the lost and corrupted body. And for confirmation of this occult doctrine he refers us to a strange feat of chemical magic which Paracelsus had recorded, and which Browne seems to credit: namely, the revival of a plant into stalk and leaves out of its burnt ashes. For the forms, he declares, are not destroyed, but are "withdrawn into their incombustible part," and lie secure from the flames.[38] In like manner the forms of dead bodies do not "wholly quit their mansions, but retire and contract themselves into their secret and inaccessible parts," until at the voice of God they rise up to be reunited with the souls that were torn from them. Finally, as the peak of this mysticism, he advances the opinion that if man survives, annihilation of the world is a mere figment of imagination, "for man subsisting, who is, and will then truly appear, a microcosm, the world cannot be said to be destroyed. For the eyes of God, and perhaps also of our glorified selves, shall as really behold and contemplate the world, in its epitome or contracted essence, as now it doth at large and in its dilated substance." [39] For what is potential is actually existent to God, who sees the leaves, flowers, and fruit in the seed.

Of course this is pure idealism. One feels that successively in terms of the philosopher's stone, the form beneath the ashes of the burnt plant, the power of God to hold the world in idea as exhibited in the microcosm, Browne is carried into a mystic region where the body and the material universe itself is simply a subjective phase of spiritual life, without any real or independent existence. The almost unescapable implication is that in the end all is absorbed into God. Browne rests at last in the conviction that "he only is; all others have an existence with dependency, and are something but by a distinction." [40] "All that is truly amiable is God, or as it were a divided piece of him, that retains a reflex or shadow of himself." [41] In short, the steady drift of these last pages is in the direction of the mystical and occult philosophies,

[37] *Ibid.*   [38] I, 48.   [39] I, 50.   [40] I, 35.   [41] II, 14.

and the thought overflows, as all powerfully imaginative thought must, any narrowly anthropomorphic conceptions of the creator and his creation.

What conceptions of nature, then, are revealed in the flashing, cryptic pages of *Religio Medici*? Obviously, among the complex elements of Christian philosophy, the ones which Browne finds most congenial are the Platonic, and these he seems to absorb for the most part from Cabbalist and Hermetical sources. In a sense the union of Christianity and Platonism in him brings him very close to the Cambridge Platonist kind of thought, but there are clear differences, and the relation is at most a broad one. Browne is much more of a mystic than any of these men except Henry More. Of the two, Browne is by far the greater, but they have points in common. They have the same fondness for alchemy, for symbolism, for spiritistic phenomena, and much the same poetic tendencies. But Browne thinks characteristically in terms of the apparent as the symbol of the real, of essence beneath accident, of the whole contracted in the part, of the divine adumbration, rather than in the Cambridge Platonist terms of a dull plastic nature in which reason embodies itself. The opposition of mechanism to mind scarcely touches him. It never occurs to him seriously that it is possible to deny that "this visible fabric" must have had a designer, and a universe without personality would be for him intolerable and meaningless. To what extent he thinks of nature as a plastic or evolutionary process is not indicated as yet. It seems clear, however, that he has little tendency to think of nature as working from within, and as for the ultimate problem of matter, he does not raise it. He is content to say that God made it out of nothing. He is convinced that natural law is not uniform and human life still less so. None the less, he contrives to vitalize these bare, teleological modes of thought. The world presents itself to him as an organism in which man and phenomenal nature exhibit an all-embracing unity and the whole in every part.

V

How, in the next place, did Browne carry on these conceptions into *Vulgar Errors* and *The Garden of Cyrus*? With the heterogeneous mass of scientific opinions of one sort and another in

Vulgar Errors we have no concern; our object is simply to draw attention to those passages which throw some special light on his natural philosophy as a whole. From that point of view, our interest in *Vulgar Errors* may be limited to some six or seven scattered passages which furnish the link between *Religio Medici* and *The Garden of Cyrus*. The thread of philosophy is those ideas of the unity of life, of the whole in the parts, of the plastic principle of nature which Browne carries all through these books, in much the same way and in the same terms, to its climax in *The Garden of Cyrus*.

There are certain foreshadowings of *The Garden of Cyrus* in *Religio Medici*. The symbolism of circle and shadow, and of the microcosm where mind and matter cross comes to be the dominant pattern of the later book. There is a note of anticipation in those early phrases about the "universal and public manuscript" and the flowers of nature from which Browne did not disdain to "suck divinity"; and again in the following stray digression that had crept into his remarks about reading character in faces: "I hold, moreover, that there is a phytognomy, or physiognomy, not only of men, but of plants and vegetables; and in every one of them some outward figures which hang as signs or bushes of their inward forms. The finger of God hath left an inscription upon all his works, not graphical, or composed of letters, but of their several forms, constitutions, parts, and operations, which, aptly joined together, do make one word that doth express their natures. By these letters God calls the stars by their names; and by this alphabet Adam assigned to every creature a name peculiar to its nature." [42] Already he has his eye on this vintner's bush that is hung out over the "vegetable shop," as he calls it years later. It is to inspire his most curious and elaborate excursion into symbolism.

We found in *Religio Medici* a scholastic blend of Moses and Aristotle and Trismegistus, plus certain solitary flashes of original thought. These flashes keep lighting up the twilight grove of *Religio Medici*; they throw glints of light too into the tedious and sandy stretches of *Vulgar Errors*. Take for example the opening chapter of Book II, where he is combatting the notion that crys-

[42] *Religio Medici*, II, 2.

tallization is congealed ice. Much of this is in the direction of sound science, and when we remember Bacon's rudimentary theory in *The New Atlantis* that crystallization can be brought about simply by burying minerals in caves, Browne seems at least up to date. He thinks that crystal is a mineral owing its nature partly to the coldness of the earth, partly to "the hand of its concretive spirit, the seeds of petrifaction and *Gorgon* within itself." This might be taken as a poetic metaphor for the modern theory of crystallization, but Browne is plainly thinking in terms of hylozoism. Minerals contain "lapidifical spirits," and therefore, although Moses says nothing about minerals, "yet is there unquestionably, a very large classis of creatures in the earth, far above the condition of elementarity." They are not plants, but nevertheless they are "determined by seminalities, that is, created and defined seeds committed unto the earth from the beginning." [43] Plainly Browne is ranging far afield for some starting point of life.

Again, in the midst of a half-scientific disquisition on the loadstone, in which he follows Gilbert to a certain extent, we suddenly come to a remarkable passage in which he seems willing to entertain the theory of a Spanish Jesuit that the human body is a magnet, and, if floated on water, will point to the north. What more likely than that the microcosm, or vegetables too for that matter, should have this mysterious property? "This opinion confirmed would much advance the microcosmical conceit, and commend the geography of Paracelsus, who according to the cardinal points of the world, divideth the body of man; and, therefore working upon human ordure, and by long preparation rendering it odoriferous, he terms it *zibeta occidentalis,* western civet; making the face the east, but the posteriors the America or western part of his microcosm." [44] This fantastic passage is typical of the book. Science is a shadowy, pathless, faerie region, in which the mystic and the occult philosopher walk side by side with the experimental investigator. The inanimate world is not yet dehumanized. In the same chapter, Browne personifies loadstone and steel — "If in two skiffs of cork, a loadstone and steel be placed within the orb of their activities, the one doth not move, the

[43] *Vulgar Errors,* II, i.
[44] *Ibid.,* II, iii.

other standing still, but both hoist sail and steer unto each other ... for in this action ... they mutually approach and run into each other's arms." [45] This language is not mere metaphor. Bacon, with a like feeling for the "soul" in things, might have said it as well.

The passage on the glowworm[46] is a remarkable example of the same sort of thing. Nothing in Browne shows more of the peculiar color of this combination of science and mysticism. He is drawn to the problem of phosphorescence. What is this mysterious cold light of the glowworm, which Cardan and others said could be distilled into a perpetual illumination? Browne has found that the insects "preserved in fresh grass have lived and shined eighteen days," but he is convinced that the light goes out with their lives, for it seems to "act but dependently on their forms." He seems, however, to find some attraction in the then popular theory of vitalism — that the soul is a fluid film, perhaps luminous, that pervades the body. "Now whether the light of animals, which do not occasionally shine from contingent causes, be of kin unto the light of heaven; whether the invisible flame of life received in a convenient matter, may not become visible, and the diffused aethereal light make little stars by conglobation in idoneous parts of the compositum: whether also it may not have some original in the seed and spirit analogous unto the element of stars, whereof some glimpse is observable in the little refulgent humor, at the first attempts of formation: philosophy may yet enquire." Ancient philosophy, he reflects, had held stars to be living creatures whose light depended on their lives, and, with a Shelley-like fancy, he muses on the possible link between these two — the invisible flame of life which their forms may render visible. It is interesting to note that this passage first appears in the third edition, in the creative year of 1658. It seems to belong to that year, not only for the echo of the phrase, "the invisible flame of life" in *Urn Burial,* but for the bond of kindred fancy that links it to *The Garden of Cyrus.*

The mystery of nature's processes arrests his attention in another way on the next page. It is in connection with the extreme

[45] *Ibid.*
[46] *Ibid.,* III, xxvii, 12.

vitality of seeds. Ants scarcely kill them when they gnaw off the grain; they are blown and floated about, but survive under all manner of conditions. Where does the power of generation stop? "The forms of things may lie deeper than we conceive them; seminal principles may not be dead in the divided atoms of plants; but wandering in the ocean of nature, when they hit upon proportionable materials, may unite, and return to their visible selves again." It is a characteristic stroke of imagination — the naturalist arrested and overwhelmed by the conviction that he cannot touch the point of life, that it is a stream.

This is not to say that Browne envisages anything like a protoplasmic germ or point of life. While Harvey was slowly evolving his great formula *omne vivum ex ovo*, Sir Thomas Browne was toiling on the patristic chapters of *Vulgar Errors* like Plato's man in the cave, often rejecting an old half truth to fall into a later whole absurdity or a fantastic theory of his own invention, and without any clear principles that would help him to choose between them. So when the ever recurrent problem reappears once more in his chapter on the Beginning of the World, he retreats as usual into a bit of scholastic obscurantism about Adam's lost rib. Matter was made out of nothing and we are all the seed of Adam, on the authority of Moses. The Greek theory, then, of the eternity of matter is wrong. So also is the old Egyptian notion that man came out of the slime, as well as the boast of the primitive Greeks that they were *autochthones* — sprung out of the earth. There never was any *autochthon* but Adam, for (and this is the true Browne) even Eve's production "was in a manner seminal; for if in every part from whence the seed doth flow, there be contained the idea of the whole; there was a seminality and contracted Adam in the rib, which by the information of a soul, was individuated unto Eve." [47] This is carrying the idea of the microcosm to the scholastic logical limit.

One more illustration will suffice. In the course of this heterogeneous rambling book, we come to a chapter on the blackness of negroes.[48] It proves to be merely the starting point for what ideas Browne has on the subject of the variety of species, and the mys-

[47] *Ibid.*, VI, i.
[48] *Ibid.*, VI, x.

tery, so puzzling then, of their distribution throughout the earth. This leads off into the bypath of the science of color. His reasons for rejecting the traditionally assigned causes of black skins — the curse of God on Cham and the heat of the sun — are modern enough to arouse no little attention. We find him speaking of "mutation" and inherited traits almost in a Darwinian way, and his pointing out the doubtful esthetics of despising black is very interesting. It is in connection with the theory of color, a subject which he thinks the savants "have left our endeavors to grope them out by twilight, and by darkness almost to discover that whose existence is evidenced by light," that we find him again musing on the protean changes of nature. Why is grass green? Why do plants with white milk and white roots grow colored flowers? These speculations are to be started again in *The Garden of Cyrus*. He has seen the white spawn of frogs and lobsters gradually darken to the color of the tadpole or the shell. There must be some grand secret of these unfolding accidents in the sperm itself, if one could trace it. "And thus," he is willing to hazard, "may it also be in the generation and sperm of negroes; that being first and in its naturals white, but upon separation of parts, accidents before invisible become apparent; there arising a shadow or dark efflorescence in the outside; whereby not only their legitimate and timely births, but their abortions are also dusky, before they have felt the scorch and fervor of the sun." Truly the strangest of all subjects to invest with rhetoric!

It has been urged[49] that the tendency to belittle Browne's scientific attainments has been overindulged; that if he is out of his depth as a universal *savant*, yet in his own professional field, as a physician, he is well up to date, and that his letters, though few, clearly bear this out. It is also pointed out that *Vulgar Errors* went into several editions in Browne's lifetime and was translated into four modern languages within a century, and that it was warmly praised by important men like Robert Boyle and others. There is a good deal in all this, but the fact remains that *Vulgar Errors* is more a repository of "the floating and inventive curiosity" of the age than a contribution to knowledge. Harvey said shrewdly that Bacon wrote science "like a Lord Chancellor";

[49] By Leroy. See especially *op. cit.*, p. 232.

he might have said that Browne wrote it like a rhapsodic monk. Browne upset many a classical authority, but, after all, he read too cautiously and respectfully to think boldly, and he sees everything through a cloud of mystical emotion. He never quite reaches the scientist's point of view. His enthusiasm for truth is not steady and cool, but always lyrical. That "unreclaimed and haggard reason" of his too often loses itself in the sun. Not that he is simply a poet strayed into science. For he is infinitely laborious and plodding and capable of the dullest scholastic tabulations and citations. Long stretches of *Vulgar Errors* are as tedious and arid as almost any patristic book that could be mentioned, and as utterly at sea intellectually. In fact, nature compounded in him very nearly equal parts of the laborious pedant, the naturalist, and the mystical poet. The poetry has proved to be the philosopher's stone that transmutes much though not all of the lump to gold, but it is gold for the poet's not the scientist's purse. The reader who pursues the quest of a natural philosophy from *Religio Medici* into *Vulgar Errors* finds soon enough that he has not left divinity for science. There is little science there. There is only a certain flush of it — the activity of a mind that is just on the point of realizing nature's plastic powers in the modern way. He has not the energy to seize this Proteus and make him change shape before his eyes.

VI

Between *Vulgar Errors* and *The Garden of Cyrus,* Browne kept a literary silence of twelve years. In the course of them English life had foamed and surged over its banks and spread out into all manner of political and scientific changes. There is practically no hint of either upheaval in *The Garden of Cyrus.* Sir Thomas, with serene calm, produces, along with *Urn Burial,* a mystical little fantasy on the quincuncial arrangement of trees as practiced by the ancients. As far as its theme is concerned, the work is partly a *tour de force* of antiquarian learning, partly pure delight in inventing the variations to such an air. In the dedication to Nicholas Bacon, he says quaintly that "the field of knowledge hath been so traced, it is hard to spring anything new." He expresses the hope, none the less, that the proffered book may be a byway untrodden even by his learned friend; if not, Browne has "missed his intention." One ventures to believe at this distance of centuries that Sir Thomas did not miss it. So he sends out his garden book in the last years of Cromwell's rule, confiding to Sir Nicholas Bacon as a fellow gardener that "in garden delights 'tis not easy to hold a mediocrity," protesting gracefully that the book is not an incongruous companion piece to *Urn Burial* "since the delightful world comes after death, and paradise succeeds the grave," and, in a gravely courteous salutation, wishing "unto this ill-judging age" a portion of Bacon's generosity and even judgment. The phrase is one of his very rare commentaries on the times.

It is a singular book, indeed, but a fascinating and beautiful one. More than that, it has aspects which are too seldom pointed out. It completes the symbolism of the other works, and at its highest points of inspiration seems to interpret those symbols in terms of the real life of nature. It is certainly bookish, like all Browne's writings, but it seems to brood over a half-disclosed secret whose splendor calls out the most magnificent passages he ever wrote.

Unquestionably in many ways this work is its author's most difficult and provokingly bizarre production. It is a very prickly burr. It is a garden book and has a delightful history, as all who recall its associations with Evelyn's diary and his correspondence with Browne will remember, but our author seems to be mainly a book gardener whose primary interest is in antiquity, metaphysics, number symbolism, and the strangest bit of Pythagoreanism in all Plato. As for the quincunx, every one knows Coleridge's protest that the book finds "quincunxes in heaven above, quincunxes in earth below, quincunxes in the mind of man, quincunxes in tones, in optic nerves, in roots of trees, in leaves, in everything." We might reply that this ought not to be a difficult thing to do, considering that the figure X, which is the essential feature of the quincunx, certainly can be found in almost anything in the universe. Anyone will admit, however, that Browne rides the quincunx to the farthest edge of thought. Gosse is right when he calls this a "radically bad book." But on many a page there are exquisite, vital observations of small things in nature, made with a botanist's care, and out of the quincunx maze he goes into a conception of plant life that leads us farther than anything else of his into the secret hiding place of life itself, the shadowy realm of being and becoming, light and darkness, rest and change.

In a subsidiary way *The Garden of Cyrus* has a real scientific interest. The strange thing is that tangled in this mass of five-point symbolism is a realization of true botanical importance, the quinary arrangement of leaves. Browne hits on a botanical principle when he says that "the greatest number of flowers consist of five leaves, and therein doth rest the settled order of nature." Again the book provoked a correspondence with his friend Henry Power which gives us the most definite information we have anywhere about Browne's actual biological theories. For the student who is interested in Browne as a scientist, it is more interesting than anything in the book itself.

A reference in *The Garden of Cyrus* to "the plastic principle" had attracted the attention of Power and he wrote to Browne for further explanation. The science of botany was of course in its infancy. Robert Hooke first discovered vegetable cells in 1665, but his work was rudimentary. Harvey's *De generatione* had been published in 1651, but he could not prove his great principle. Nothing could be done without real microscopes. The prevailing biology in those days was the so-called preformationism — the theory that the whole organism is fully formed in the seed in miniature and then simply enlarged by growth. The old theory of epigenesis — the progressive development of the parts from a single homogeneous organism — was in the air, but it was not strongly advanced until the advent of Wolfe in the late eighteenth century.

Power in his letter argues for preformationism and calls to witness the embryon plant perfect in all its parts in the seed. "The smallest seeds," he says, "are nothing but their own plants shrunk into an atom, which though invisible to us, are easily discernible to nature." [50] Browne answers cautiously.[51] He reminds Power that we cannot see the plant until its germination is advanced, but he thinks that "it is not improbable that the plant is deline-

---

[50] *Works*, VI, 290. (Wilkin, II, 518n.)
[51] *Ibid.*, 293. (Wilkin, II, 519.)

ated from the beginning, that a lineal draft beginneth upon the first separation, and that these unto the eye of nature are but so many young ones hanging upon the mother plant, very soon discoverable in some by rudimental lines in the soft, jelly-like neb, in others more plainly some time after by more plain root and leaves." He adduces "spontaneous generation" (which of course he takes for granted) — best seen in duckweed, he thinks. He has watched it minutely for three or four hours and even in the first alteration "as big as a needle's point" has seen the leaves and roots together suddenly appear. But he is not satisfied that we can see closely enough. He wonders whether, as Harvey thinks, some parts are not potentially rather than actually present at first. Perhaps, on the other hand, "they are not delineated *per epigenesia*, or one after another, but in a circle, or all together, as Hippocrates expresseth, though to be discoverable successively or one after another."

It is not necessary to pursue these speculations. The whole question was far beyond the range of seventeenth-century biology, and is not yet settled, but this exchange of letters is worth quoting for the glimpse it affords of current biological views. It is an interesting example, too, of Browne's inveterate disposition to cling to the idea of the whole in every part, as the basis of teleology. But it is time to return to the dreamy symbolism of *The Garden of Cyrus*.

"All things began in order, so shall they end, and so shall they begin again; according to the ordainer of order and mystical mathematics of the city of heaven" — this is the golden theme of the book. And Browne draws from it all the music of his magical prose. Everyone knows the wonderful last page beginning, "But the quincunx of heaven runs low." [52] For the confirmed lover of Browne, there is enchantment enough merely in the connotative effects of "the pensile or hanging garden of Babylon," the "botanical bravery" of the Persians, the very names of "Nebuchodonosor," of Ahasuerus, of Cyrus "the splendid and regular plant-

[52] In a review of Lytton Strachey's essay on Sir Thomas Browne, Mr. H. S. Canby pointed out a mistake in the famous last paragraph of *The Garden of Cyrus* which curiously enough no writer on Browne seems to have noticed. Browne writes late at night that "the huntsmen are up in America, and they are already past their first sleep in Persia." Obviously the computation of time is wrong.

er," and of the legendary Abraham who brought plants from India. Such epigrams as "gardens were before gardeners and but some hours after the earth" have a radiance and freshness not found elsewhere. And starring the sober texture of scholarship are exquisite observations of nature at close range, as, for example, of "the artichoke wherein the black and shining flies do shelter themselves, when they retire from the purple flower about it." We have here at their best all those exotic, oriental, richly somber qualities of style of which Browne was so great a master, and the last, subtle charm of it is the aromatic fragrance, as from pressed flowers, of his quaint Latinisms and old world learning.

We need not follow very far the bizarre search for the quincunx — starting with the pattern of trees planted in slanting rows so that the intersecting lines form lozenges. Browne pursues the lozenge, the five points, the cross, all of which are involved in the pattern, into the four corners of the earth. The feature of it most necessary to his symbolism, however, is the decussation or intersection — the four corners and cross in the middle — which "makes up the letter X, that is, the emphatical decussation or fundamental figure." He seems to consider this endless Pythagorean excursion a very modest one. He will "decline the old theme of crosses and crucifixions," we are assured at the outset, but he lingers a moment on it nevertheless, with the antiquarian's reluctance to put away such a temptation. Later on after the lozenge idea has germinated beyond our hopes into a really powerful symbolism, he cannot resist adding the anticlimactic fifth chapter for the sake of a last flight of virtuosity on the number five. For though "to enlarge this contemplation unto all the mysteries and secrets, accomodable unto this number, were inexcusable Pythagoreanism," still it were well to remind the gentle reader that five was the number of justice, the conjugal number, the number of generation (the letter E, the fifth, being a necessary addition to Abraham's name before he could be fertile); that the fifth day saw the most numerous creation and the largest blessing; that five is the spherical number; that it "makes up the mystical name of God, which consisting of letters denoting all the spherical numbers, ten, five, and six, emphatically sets forth the notion of Trismegistus, and that intelligible sphere, which is the nature of God."

There is page on page of this patristic and rabbinical lore. It makes the brain swirl as organ fugues did Lamb's, when he wrote incoherently of "Gog and Magog." Sir Thomas has a lofty disdain of "crambe verities and questions over-queried." "Flat and flexible truths are beat out by every hammer; but Vulcan and his whole forge sweat to work out Achilles his armor." The field of the quincunx is white unto the harvest, he thinks. The botanists of the future must address themselves to it and so "erect generalities, disclose unobserved proprieties, not only in the vegetable shop, but the whole volume of nature; affording delightful truths, confirmable by sense and ocular observation, which seems to me the surest path, to trace the labyrinth of truth. For though discursive enquiry and rational conjecture may leave handsome gashes and flesh-wounds; yet without conjunction of this, expect no mortal or dispatching blows unto error."

Here is Browne's scientific point of view in a nutshell. One lobe of his brain wants to study facts and test hypotheses on the basis of them, the other is fascinated by mystic symbols and analogies. That phrase "delightful truths" tells the story. It is the story of the fatal malady of Greek and patristic and Cabbalist science — the tendency to take abstractions for things, illustrations for arguments, analogies for principles. They could see resemblances but not differences, and they had that vice which Bacon considered one of the chief idols of the tribe — the inordinate habit of reading more unity into things than the facts justified. One of the worst results, all through the history of philosophy, was the disease of allegorizing. But the thing was dying out in the seventeenth century, and Browne's naive search for "delightful truths" in *The Garden of Cyrus* was no longer really respectable in science.

For a parallel to it in a writer of any real reputation, we have to unearth Henry More's *Antidote against Atheism*, or his *Conjectura Cabbalistica*, works which show the insidious decline of a fine mind. The former work has quaint resemblances to *The Garden of Cyrus*, and will illustrate as well as anything the method of that medieval botany that could still cast its spell over mystics. The form, beauty, seed, and signature of plants, says More, are arguments of Providence. A few plants have marks to show their use, like the inscriptions on apothecaries' boxes; not all, for that would be harping on one string, and man had to use his wits to find out the uses of the others, but there are inscriptions on some legible enough even for him who runs. The maidenhair is an example. Its lye is good for baldness! Walnuts look like the head — their salts are good for head wounds! "Thus did divine Providence by natural hieroglyphics read short physic lectures to the rude wit of man." The answer to the question why some plants, geraniums for example, do not resemble anything pertaining to physic is very amusing. More ventures the opinion that these are "ludicrous ornaments of nature like the flourishes about a great letter, that signify nothing but are made only to delight the eye." And our first parents, far from being put out by these failures in signature reading, were only led to investigate plants that had no signatures at all, and so to discover their medicinal properties for themselves. Scientifically Browne is not so many steps in advance of this sort of thing. In the same way, if one wants a seventeenth-century parallel to the number symbolism of *The Garden of Cyrus*, More's *Conjectura Cabbalistica* will furnish it. Not Philo himself can more thoroughly squeeze the last drop of allegorical meaning out of a number.

The subject is a formidable one, and not to be launched here. Evidently we do not understand the Greeks until we realize, as More says in commenting on the Pythagorean square, that "it was not the nature and mystery of numbers, but of *things* that was comprehended in the Pythagoric Tetractys." It is an important commentary. When they said "Virtue is number," the word number certainly stood for something that we no longer feel in it. Sir Thomas Browne was under the spell of this kind of symbolism. But compared with the symbolism of Philo's *On Creation*, or the astounding lucubrations of the Rosicrucians on the symbols of the rose and the cross, or More's rhapsody on the Cabbala, *The Garden of Cyrus* is, by such standards of virtuosity, a very modest little book indeed.

One comes to feel that the really interesting significance of the book is the application of this number symbolism, so strange a marriage of Greece and Christianity, to the development of plant life. It is all built up around the notion of decussation or crossing. What started the idea in Browne's mind? It may have been a passage in Plato's *Timaeus*; it may have been the Christian Justin Martyr's commentary on that passage in his *Apology*. Both are famous in the history of the microcosmic philosophy, and in *The Garden of Cyrus* the two are introduced as the climax of the fourth chapter. The reader will make nothing of Browne's paraphrase of Plato, nor will he fare better on repairing to the *Timaeus* itself and finally to the commentaries for light on this mighty Pythagorean darkness. It seems, however, that in the *Timaeus*, the work which Jowett says "is the most obscure and repulsive to the modern reader, and has nevertheless had the greatest influence over the ancient and medieval world," Plato, groping for some symbol for the relation of mind and matter, finds it in the conception that the creator, having cut the whole mass of the universe into two strips, crossed them in the figure X and bent them around into an inner and outer circle. Spirit intersects with body and enspheres it both in the micro- and macrocosm. Then Justin Martyr, seeking confirmation of Christianity in Greek thought, imagines Plato to have borrowed the phrase *decussavit eum in universo* from Moses' story of the uplifted brazen serpent, and to have mistaken for X the letter T. The tau is *his* symbol. The incarnation is the Christian way of avoiding pantheism; it is the union of very God and very man, and the outstretched hands on the cross typify the human body stretched through the universe. Here, then, is the union of theological truth with the doctrine of the microcosm — the symbol of the psychological union of mind and matter.

A curious forgotten volume, Robert Fludd's *Utriusque Cosmi Maioris Scilicet et Minoris . . . Historia* (1617), offers a vivid presentation of this conception. The frontispiece is an engraving of the chart of the universe. In the middle is the figure of a man with arms and legs stretched out. Behind his flanks, a small disk, evidently the earth, is the center. Around it are four circles representing the four humors. A circle which touches the five points of head, fingertips, and toes, encloses him. This is the microcosm. Outside this are the Ptolemaic astronomical circles with the planets and stars fastened upon them. A cord is fixed to the primum mobile, and this is being whirled around by a winged figure which has on its head an hour glass surmounted by a mystic cross.

It seems unquestionable that this bizaare symbolism of points and intersections, in all sorts of variations, was the common medium of psychological thinking. The thing to notice is an original symbolic combination in Browne's treatment. He seems to take this mystical notion of decussation, and to combine it, after years of brooding on the line that nature traces in plants, with his favorite symbol of adumbration. One wonders whether there was ever such an ethereally delicate play of fancy on the subject of plastic nature as the resulting combination produces. In certain passages of *The Garden of Cyrus* he manages to blend the "mystical mathematics of heaven" and the mystical shadow of light discerned in flowers and trees with profound and enchanting suggestiveness.

We have seen how controlling in *Religio Medici* is the feeling for adumbration. The same feeling gives *Urn Burial* too its characteristic color. This is the symbolism of the urn, and the motto of the book, the apothegm that sets the key of its meditation, might be "Darkness and light divide the course of time." In a word, Browne is always escaping from the too, too solid earth of orthodox teleology into the bright clouds of the emanation theories. To breathe the air of this climate, one must read in Philo's *Creation* of the "incorporeal light" perceptible only to the intellect, "far more brilliant than that which is seen," that later begins to change and obscure itself into light perceptible to the senses. Or the patristic play of imagination on such a verse as *virtus altissimi obumbrabit tibi*. Or Bruno's *De umbris idearum*, built up with mystical subtlety on the text "We sat down under his shadow with great delight." Or Robert Fludd's Cabbalist exposition of the primal matter as *umbra* and *tenebrae*, "a rude, undigested, and imperceptible mass," the dark water of chaos in which unity was hidden until the light of formal being shining forth by emanation made the world, and *aleph tenebrosum* became *aleph lucidum*. So too, Browne says in the end, "The greatest mystery of religion is expressed by adumbration, and in the noblest part of Jewish types, we find the cherubims shadowing the mercy seat." [53]

Pushing through the endless citations of all the crosses and five-pointed things in the universe, we get at the heart of the book by way of two digressions. The lozenge figure is only the rough rind

---

[53] *The Garden of Cyrus*, chap. iv.

of his thought; so too are the statistics of quinary arrangement. The real approach to plastic nature is made through the observation that leaves cross each other, that nature's economy is one of enfolding or protecting. Not only so, but this process begins so far down, in the seed itself, that one can never touch the beginning of it.

Having temporarily exhausted the more obvious examples of the X pattern, he has turned for a moment from the network design in plants to comment on the fact that they put out their leaves from the stalk in different directions, regularly spaced, in such a way as to afford each other the most cunning protection. And then, led on to another digression, he pauses to observe a fact that has already held his attention in *Vulgar Errors*: "How little is required unto effectual generation, and in what diminutives the plastic principle lodgeth, is exemplified in seeds, wherein the greater mass affords so little comproduction." [54] So little is really vital; the life spark is in a tiny nib; and moreover, it is impossible to tell whether the root or leaf starts first — "they seem to start and set out upon one signal of nature."

It is his absorption in this plastic point of seeds, wherein life seems to be "delineated in a circle," as he told Henry Power, that starts the train of speculation leading to the magnificent close of the fourth chapter. He has seen how in muddy water "if the first and rudimental strokes of duckweed be observed, the leaves and roots anticipate not each other," but seem to start together. Nature's processes are too deep, too minute for any eye to follow — "the seminal powers lie in great part invisible, while the sun finds polypody in stone walls." [55] Seeds, he finds too, are marvellously long-lived, and he introduces notes from his commonplace books[56] on that fact, echoes too from *Vulgar Errors*, for he has long been meditating on the secret of that fecundity which "wanders through the ocean of nature," of that deep life which persists "in the divided atoms of plants." [57] What is this plastic principle? He knows little more about it than Culverwel, who said that it could "admit a soul very agreeably," or than Henry More, who

[54] Chap. iii.
[55] *Ibid.*
[56] Cf. *Works*, V, 334. (Wilkin, III, 382.)
[57] *Vulgar Errors*, III, xxvii, 13.

declared there were six stages of seminal life from ethereal to terrestrial. Is Paracelsus right in imagining that bodies were first spirits, Browne asks? Or Aristotle, with his theory that the link between earth and spirit is water? He finds much in the first watery liquor, in the "diaphanous jelly before deeper incrassation" to warrant this idea.[58] He recurs, too, to the mysterious power of spontaneous generation which, as he supposed, bred insects on trees and dead bodies and even live fish. Presently he returns to the subject in a paragraph of dreamy meditation on the variety of motions to be observed in plants — "The summer-worm of ponds and plashes makes a long waving motion; the hair-worm seldom lies still." Are not these almost animate motions?

It seems a wandering way to pursue the quincunx idea. And the beginning of the fourth chapter is unpromising. "As for the delights, commodities, mysteries, with other concernments of this order," it begins, "we are unwilling to fly them over, in the short deliveries of Virgil, Varro, or others, and shall therefore enlarge with additional ampliations." Scholastic learning seems to be getting its second wind. Then follows a recital of the aforesaid advantages of planting in quincunx formation — that it gives proper room for expansion, affords the most sun and wind, allows trees to breathe and feed through their leaves, and so forth.

And then suddenly in a way which one comes to look for in Browne, we feel the first breath of heightening imagination. Trees in this pattern are like the columniation in old porticoes and temples, the inspiration for which, indeed, men first took from rows of trees. They give prospect and shade. The sight "being not diffused, but circumscribed between long parallels and adumbrations from the branches, it frameth a penthouse over the eye, and maketh a quiet vision," as a man hollows his hand above his eyes. "And therefore Providence hath arched and paved the great house of the world, with colors of mediocrity, that is, blue and green, above and below the sight, moderately terminating the *acies* of the eye."

He is working toward his poetic climax. He may be no nearer to laying open the secret of nature's processes, but he has an esthetic theory that satisfies him. This crossing and enfolding

[58] *The Garden of Cyrus*, chap. iii.

from seed to overarching tree is the method of the art of God. It is infinitely cunning and subtle art. We cannot trace the chemical change that turns the white below ground, "the candor of their seminal pulp," to the green above, nor stop nature at any point in the process; water, "the alimental vehicle of plants," when life begins in it, turns green imperceptibly. But the art of green color is there. Not only so, but shadows are contrived "through the great volume of nature" whereby plants shade and protect themselves and others, leaves shadowing stock and root, calicular petals inclosing the flowers, the flowers wrapped about the seeds. Deeper still, seeds themselves are wrapped in the impenetrable shadow of protective coverings. The idea is elementary in its simplicity, but Browne suddenly unfolds all its philosophical implications in a few truly magnificent sentences. They seem the finest he ever wrote.

"But seeds themselves do lie in perpetual shades, either under the leaf, or shut up in coverings; and such as lie barest have their husks, skins, and pulps about them, wherein the neb and generative particle lieth moist and secured from the injury of air and sun. Darkness and light hold interchangeable dominions, and alternately rule the seminal state of things. Light unto Pluto is darkness unto Jupiter. Legions of seminal ideas lie in their second chaos and Orcus of Hippocrates; till putting on the habits of their forms, they show themselves upon the stage of the world, and open dominion of Jove. They that held the stars of heaven were but rays and flashing glimpses of the empyreal light, through holes and perforations of the upper heaven, took off the natural shadows of stars, while according to better discovery the poor inhabitants of the moon have but a polary life, and must pass half their days in the shadow of that luminary.

"Light that makes things seen, makes some things invisible; were it not for darkness and the shadow of the earth, the noblest part of the creation had remained unseen, and the stars in heaven as invisible as on the fourth day, when they were created above the horizon, with the sun, or there was not an eye to behold them. The greatest mystery of religion is expressed by adumbration, and in the noblest part of Jewish types, we find the cherubims shadowing the mercy seat. Life itself is but the shadow of death, and souls departed but the shadows of the living. All things fall under this name. The sun itself is but the dark simulacrum, and light but the shadow of God." [59]

This voluminous music is the final, major resolution of Browne's theme. His books are not held together by any framework of logical thought, but taken as parts of a whole they have the esthetic unity of musical material developed from one movement to another. The themes are the persistent symbols of the mystic circle of God, of the figure X, and of the adumbration of light, which he sounds again and again in many forms and combinations.

The conclusions we have reached may be indicated in a few words. Sir Thomas Browne is, of course, very little of a scientist. He may have realized dimly with Bacon that it was not possible to make "Proteus ever change shape until he was straitened and held fast," but he was not capable of this arduous endeavor. He did nothing to control nature, nothing to advance the scientific determination of nature's laws. If he could have had a far glimpse into the future, he might have agreed with Cardinal Newman that the fruit of the tree of science is magical but poisonous, for he cared rather to worship nature's mysteries than to plunder her treasures and harness her forces. He read the "universal and public manuscript" as mystics and poets always read it — for its haunting whispers of ideal beauty and truth. His was the quest of the changeless, and he pursued it through rigid theological formulas and dry and absurd symbols and dizzy paradoxes with an energy and imagination that at scattered points managed to vitalize almost all of them. No doubt his poetic gifts and intellectual force are mixed with much chaff of dusty learning, rhetorical extravagances, fantastic symbolism pursued to absurdity and tediousness, and patristic dullness and credulity. Often he falls under the accusation that Emerson brings against Swedenborg, that he turns symbols into bloodless abstractions, and those who sit at the feet of the mystics probably feel little heat in the smoldering fire of his ideas, and might even dismiss them, as Miss Evelyn Underhill dismisses the ideas of the Cambridge Platonists, as "tepid speculations." Many of his admirers have thought otherwise, and for

[59] *Ibid.*, chap. iv.

THE ART OF GOD

them Sir Thomas Browne penetrates as far as words can reach into the dim realm of being and becoming, past change itself to

> That same time when no more change shall be,
> But steadfast rest of all things, firmly staid
> Upon the pillars of eternity,
> That is contrair to Mutability.

The art of God, which is the mystery of becoming, he traces at last in the burning bush of nature herself, and quietly contemplates the creative light that lies in stars and flowers underneath the enveloping shadows of the phenomenal world.

CHAPTER IV

That Great Amphibium

"WE ARE only that amphibious piece between a corporal and spiritual essence, that middle form that links those two together, and makes good the method of God and nature, that jumps not from extremes, but unites the incompatible distances by some middle and participating natures. . . . Thus is man that great and true amphibium, whose nature is disposed to live, not only like other creatures in divers elements, but in divided and distinguished worlds."[1]

"Thus we are men, and we know not how: there is something in us that can be without us, and will be after us; though it is strange that it hath no history what it was before us, nor cannot tell how it entered in us."[2]

I

The last chapter undertook to explain Sir Thomas Browne's conception of the nature of things, of how God created and how he sustains the fabric of the universe, or macrocosm. We may turn now in more detail to what he has to say about the microcosm, or inner world of man. Man, as Browne thinks of him, is a world in himself, for he alone unites in his being the whole range of ele-

---

[1] *Religio Medici*, I, 34.
[2] *Ibid.*, I, 36.

ments and faculties in the universe, he alone is the meeting place of all its stages of reality. He combines matter and spirit, that is, he has a body and a soul. The question is, what is the soul and how is it united with the body?

The traditional arguments for the existence of the soul, such as the Genesis story of special creation, the appeal to the higher powers of man to think, to will, to develop moral attributes, to aspire to immortality, to conceive of God, the inability of material combinations to account for mind — all these were partly speculative and partly religious. But they were purely deductive, for they had no biological knowledge to support them. This is not to suggest that the mystery of life has now been solved by modern science or that the question of the soul has been disposed of. But the seventeenth century was altogether unripe for psychology. It knew as little of the body as of the soul. Physiology, in any modern sense, made its real beginnings only in the sixteenth century, and the birth of the biological sciences as a whole was late and their infancy extremely prolonged.

The Christian tradition has always been steadily committed to the doctrine that human personality can be explained only on the basis of an inorganic, immortal soul, temporarily inhabiting but entirely separable from the body. This idea has always involved baffling complications, for even the very earliest psychologists were forced to see that personality is an organic whole and cannot be separated into parts. The mechanistic philosophy which held that spirit is simply the finest atoms did not solve the ultimate problems of life and intelligence, but it was at least fairly unified. When Plato, however, split the universe into mind and matter, soul and body, he introduced an irreconcilable dualism. Aristotle, far more conscious than Plato of the unity of all life, rejected the Platonic idealism, and taught instead that every existing body is a concrete whole, composed of matter, on the one hand, and on the other of "form," which is different from matter. But this distinction between matter and form unescapably carries on the same dualism. Christian theologians, who inherited this dualistic psychology of Plato and Aristotle, were helpless to explain the interaction of these supposedly separate entities. Following the classical philosophers, they divided the soul into parts — such as the vegetative, sensitive, and rational souls — but they realized too well that such a method of explaining the human mechanism is a rude and clumsy one. On the one hand, they had adopted, as alone compatible with Christianity, the Platonic doctrine of an immortal soul confined temporarily to the prison house of the body; on the other, they realized with Aristotle the organic unity of mind and matter. But Aristotle's psychology is extremely obscure. The soul is the "entelechy" or "form" of the body, he says, but how the two are related he cannot explain. He resorts to various metaphors: it may be as the wax to the seal, or the vision to the eye, or the sailor to the ship. The one thing that Aristotle is clear about is his denial of personal immortality, and very consistently he binds up the reason into the body along with all the lower faculties. But this is the very doctrine that Christianity could not accept.

In the thirteenth century, Thomas Aquinas attempted a final statement of the Christian doctrine of the soul.[3] He accepts the Platonic doctrine of the immaterial and immortal soul, but he rejects Plato's radical dualism and adopts instead a modification of Aristotelian psychology to accommodate it to Christian doctrine. He insists that there is one substance in man, the self or the ego, and that the soul is the vital principle of the body as well as of the mind. But there is a higher, an "active" part of the soul, whose functions are thought and volition, and that is dependent alone on the divine intellect and derived from God only. Though all parts of the soul are united in one substance, the self, and are the "form" of the body, yet the soul is immortal and separable from the body. The embryo has the lower forms of the soul; the rational soul is created at birth. So the soul is, after all, a spiritual substance, different in nature from the body, and, though directing its processes, only temporarily associated with it. St. Thomas, in other words, perpetuates, and in fact in a more extreme form, the dualism of Aristotelian psychology.

The physiology behind these doctrines was, of course, very crude, for neither Aristotle nor Galen nor St. Thomas could possibly have an adequate knowledge of the human body. Galen, it is true, had begun to dissect, and had accumulated a remarkable

---

[3] *Summa Theologica*, I, Questions 75–102.

mass of anatomical information, and the Arabians and Jews had cherished the medical sciences and somewhat enlarged his discoveries, but the prejudice of the Church against dissection of the human body kept physiology at a standstill through long centuries well into the Renaissance. Physiology, in any real sense, began only in the sixteenth century, when Vesalius, Fabrizio, Rivière, Harvey, and van Helmont for the first time made a searching study of the body. All these men made dissections, Vesalius by stealth, the others more and more under the protection of the State. Vesalius found no essential differences between the brains of animals and men, and seems, as far as he dared, to have been a materialist. And though he inherited the accepted physiology of the day — of the natural spirits made by the liver, the vital spirits by the heart, and the animal spirits by the brain — he began a revolt against the paralyzing dominance of Galen.

Sir Thomas Browne, after going through the old-fashioned Oxford course of medical readings in Hippocrates and Galen, without dissections or clinical practice, intelligently decided to find something better. He went to the Continent, and there he was immediately thrown into new and stimulating currents — at Montpelier under Rivière, at Padua under disciples of Vesalius, at Leyden possibly under van Helmont. He may still have been taught that the soul is a vital principle diffused through the body, but he saw dissections, and he learned at first hand some of the rudiments of organic chemistry. Later in life he embraced whole-heartedly Harvey's discovery of the circulation of the blood, the one revolutionary principle of his generation that he fully understood, and when his son Edward began to lecture at the Royal College of Physicians, we find Browne contributing active help. He was an indefatigable student of anatomy, and urged his young disciple Power to make it his "fidus Achates."

In the early seventeenth century, as a matter of fact, the older metaphysical dualism had already been destroyed by Bacon, for the effect of his method was to show that in nature the word "form" can only mean a law of the action of matter. It followed that the psychology of Aristotle and St. Thomas was rendered impossible, for if the soul is the "form" of the body, it can be nothing but a mode of matter, and this is simply materialism. It was possible for a few years to adopt Bacon's cautious procedure of separating the "natural" from the "revealed" and to say that the "sensitive" soul is earthly, the "rational" divine and not to be studied except by theology. But this method proved less satisfactory in psychology than in physics, since the study of man involves examining the mind in union, here on earth, with the body, as St. Thomas himself knew. As a matter of fact, psychology is perhaps Bacon's weakest point. It was possible, again, to banish psychology from the field as unripe for discussion, and confine attention to mechanical phenomena, as the Royal Society did. But for most men, especially the religious-minded, the soul was the most fascinating and important of subjects and the center of intellectual excitement. Unripe the science certainly was, and it had to wait until very recent years for even the rudiments of a scientific method. But though these seventeenth-century speculations were very crude, scientists and philosophers had sufficient data to perceive many of the problems involved, and they used lines of argument which are still being advanced.

In Shakespeare's day the *De proprietatibus rerum* of Bartholomew, as translated by Batman (1582) under the title *Batman upon Bartholomew,* was the popular natural history. We find there all the older psychology in its quaintest form, presented of course in terms of the microcosm, under which conception the science of man involved the study of the stars, the planetary signs, the four elements, the four humors, and the three divisions of the soul. This venerable physiology and psychology, surviving today chiefly in the chart on the almanac, was the serious scientific basis of *The Fairy Queen,* Davies' *Nosce Teipsum,* Burton's *Anatomy,*[4] the *Novum Organum,* Fletcher's *Purple Island, Paradise Lost,* and *Religio Medici.* In general, all these works adopt the same divisions of the brain, the same notion of the kinds of spirits, the same threefold soul. And they carry down from the Greeks the same symbols for these souls. "His similitude," Browne says, referring to Aristotle, "of a triangle comprehended in a square doth somewhat illustrate the trinity of our souls, and that the triple unity of God; for there is in us, if not three dis-

---

[4] The seventeenth-century doctrine of the soul is fully illustrated in Burton's *Anatomy of Melancholy* (1621), Pt. I, Sec. 1, mem. 2, subs. 5 ff.

tinct souls, yet differing faculties, that can and do subsist apart in different subjects, and yet in us are so united as to make but one soul and substance." [5] The symbols he refers to are the same that Spenser uses in the description of the House of Temperance,[6] and Fletcher in *The Purple Island*,[7] and Bartholomew explains them for us. The symbol of the vegetative soul, he says, is the triangle, because it has the three powers of self-sustainment, growth and reproduction; that of the sensitive soul is the square, for various occult reasons, but chiefly because its powers are common sense, imagination, reason, and memory; the rational soul is the perfect circle.

But even while some of the later of these works were being written, and during the young manhood of Browne, the Cartesian philosophy, as well as Bacon's, was rapidly undermining the entire scholastic structure. Descartes' bare and sharp dualism between thought and extension revolutionized the old conceptions, and brought into clear view the problems of psychology in a way that changed the course of all future studies. He was convinced that life does not need to be explained by "soul," that everything but thought is purely mechanical, and he rejected the theory of the diffused psychic principle, denied the existence of a vegetative and sensitive soul either in man or animals, the classical bridge between the animate and the inanimate, and adopted instead the atomist theory of the older Greeks — that life and movement are due to "animal spirits," or purely material atoms. These spirits are simply the finest particles of the blood, filtered from the arteries through minute pores into the brain and thence into the nerves. The body is a machine pure and simple. But man, and man alone, is a thinking being, and this thought substance lodges somehow in the body and interacts with it. Man, therefore, has an incorporeal soul, but its sole function is thought, and it has a definite seat in the brain, in fact, he said (making an unfortunate guess), in the pineal gland of the brain. Such a psychology, which can allow only this dubious and minute point of contact between thought and matter, was unsatisfactory enough, but it had the merit of raising the

[5] *Religio Medici*, I, 12.
[6] *The Fairy Queen*, II. ix.
[7] *The Purple Island*, Canto I, 44.

sharpest possible issues in the next generation, and the greatest thinkers of the period formulated doctrines which were to guide all the controversies of the eighteenth century.

Perhaps no department of seventeenth-century knowledge seems so crudely rudimentary and naive as the psychological, and for that reason the modern reader derives nine parts of amusement to one of edification from the perusal of *The Purple Island*, or even *Nosce Teipsum*. "Know thyself" was the popular watchword, the open sesame of the moment. But on the lips of amateur philosophers and pious clergymen, quite stultified in their adherence to the grand old regime, the slogan has its comic pathos. The labored arguments of Davies and the bland exposition of Fletcher seem less respectable intellectually than any other kind of output of the day. The Reverend Daniel Featly delivered the following pompous sentiment in his introduction to *The Purple Island*: "He that would learn theology must first study autology. The way to God is by ourselves: it is a blind and dirty way; it hath many windings, and is easy to be lost; this poem will make thee understand that way." This is quaintly oracular to an uncommon degree, largely because neither the learned eulogist nor the learned poet could possibly have enterd a field of knowledge in which he was more profoundly ignorant, or in which greater changes were to take place. When Browne loftily declines the study of the tides, the increase of Nilus, and the conversion of the needle, that he may devote his attention to the "cosmography of myself," he adopts the popular slogan. But in this field he is not exactly an amateur. If he is in front of his generation anywhere it is here, and there is after all a certain professional challenge in the title of his first book. *Religio Medici* records the first reactions of an alert mind to a cosmopolitan scientific education. He has not been content to read Galen and Hippocrates in the perfunctory medical course of Oxford, but has been in contact on the Continent with the new physiology and the mechanic philosophy. What he has to say about the soul has, therefore, a considerable interest.

II

Browne approaches the subject through the great chain or ladder of being, which "rises not disorderly or in confusion, but with a comely method and proportion," through the five stages, mineral, vegetable, animal, human, angelic, to God. At the top are the angels and these, he thinks, must have to perfection all those intellectual qualities which we possess in rudimentary form: their knowledge is intuitive rather than discursive; they know the "forms" of things — that great desideratum; they have sublimated powers of movement; they live underneath the accidents of matter, and perhaps in light.

In the middle of the scale is man, the microcosm, the "compendium," the "great amphibium" who inhabits two worlds. Browne loved to turn these conceptions over in his mind and explore their figurative possibilities. If nature is the complete manuscript, then man is the handbook;[8] or, in another figure, the man who is sufficient to himself in his little world is "above Atlas's shoulders";[9] or again, in terms of spiritual astronomy, the soul is the macrocosm and the material globe of the world a mere speck inside it;[10] or, still further, the arc of flesh that circumscribes the mind measures three hundred and sixty degrees, but the arc of the mind is unlimited, — "I take my circle to be above three hundred and sixty."[11] The womb-shaped burial urns inspire another play of fancy — a quaint biological analogy this time: "But the common form with necks was a proper figure, making our last bed like our first; nor much unlike the urns of our nativity, while we lay in the nether part of the earth, and inward vault of our microcosm."[12] Human nature is a sphere of some sort, enclosing all the elements of life in an inexplicable union.

The microcosm symbol is congenial to Browne also because it dramatizes his religious psychology. The human personality is a little world because it is the spacious and all-important scene of that battle with the devil that men once waged so earnestly in the immense solitude of the religious conscience. "There is no man alone, because every man is a microcosm, and carries the whole world about him. . . . Indeed, though in a wilderness, a

---

[8] *Religio Medici*, I, 50.
[9] Ibid., II, 11.
[10] *Ibid.*
[11] *Ibid.*
[12] *Urn Burial*, chap. iii.

man is never alone, not only because he is with himself and his own thoughts, but because he is with the devil, who ever consorts with our solitude, and is that unruly rebel that musters up those disordered motions which accompany our sequestered imaginations." [13]

Browne states the orthodox doctrine of the soul picturesquely and in words that throw into bold relief the scholastic psychology. "The whole creation is a mystery, and particularly that of man. At the blast of his mouth were the rest of the creatures made, and at his bare word they started out of nothing: but in the frame of man (as the text describes it) he played the sensible operator, and seemed not so much to create as make him. When he had separated the materials of other creatures, there consequently resulted a form and a soul; but having raised the walls of man, he was driven to a second and harder creation of a substance like himself, an incorruptible and immortal soul." [14]

But now Browne speaks with more professional confidence. Dismissing without any debate Paracelsus' claim that he could make an homunculus in his laboratory, he raises the moot question of the manner and time of the birth of the soul.[15] The rival theories were those of "traduction" and "infusion," according to the first of which the soul was inherited through the male parent, according to the second bestowed as the immediate gift of God. Browne is inclined to accept the theory of infusion, but he is haunted by an objection, "not wrung from speculations and subtleties, but from common sense and observation; not picked from the leaves of any author, but bred amongst the weeds and tares of my own brain." It develops that the objection which he thus modestly advances is based on his belief in "the equivocal and monstrous productions in the copulation of man with beast." He credits the floating stories that such monstrosities exist and that according to report they have a considerable "impression and tincture of reason." This seems to him to shake the theory of infusion, and leads him to wonder whether these amorphous creatures with their imperfect faculties do not go to prove that

[13] *Religio Medici*, II, 10.
[14] *Ibid.*, I, 36.
[15] *Ibid.*

"soul" is merely a higher and inherited organization rather than a unique divine gift. Yet this rather grim consideration does not really disturb him. It is one of those more or less aimless, pseudo-scientific queries which often seem to pop into his head, and he goes on to explain in orthodox professional terms that though the soul in her earthly estate is not altogether inorganic, but to some extent dependent on the body, and needs "not only a symmetry and proper disposition of organs, but a crasis and temper correspondent to its operations," nevertheless the body controls only the lower functions of the soul, and the pure soul is without any question inorganic and self-existing. It is, of course, useless to inquire the meaning of this learned jargon about the "symmetry" and "crasis" and "temper" of the physical organs. It cannot possibly mean anything more than that body and mind are mysteriously connected in some way which the learned physician does not at all understand. The soul may be, he thinks, like hidden gold in baser metal, or butterflies in cocoons. But he does not doubt the existence of this inorganic soul, and his dissections of the brain, far from disturbing, have only confirmed his belief. "Amongst all those rare discoveries and curious pieces I find in the fabric of man, I do not so much content myself, as in that I find not, there is no organ or instrument for the rational soul; for in the brain, which we term the seat of reason, there is not anything of moment more than I can discover in the crany of a beast: and this is a sensible and no inconsiderable argument of the inorganity of the soul." Anatomy might drive Vesalius to materialism, but it brings Browne to humble reverence, and he closes the discussion on a characteristic note of awe and wonder: "Thus we are men, and we know not how: there is something in us that can be without us, and will be after us; though it is strange that it hath no history what it was before us, nor cannot tell how it entered in us."

On the subject of the resurrection Browne appears to have entertained a variety of opinions. One of his old-fashioned heresies, we remember, had been the belief that the soul dies with the body and is revived with it at the resurrection day, but he had swung round to the orthodox view on this point and declares positively that "the souls of the faithful, as they leave earth, take possession of heaven." [16] As for ghosts and apparitions, these are not wandering souls but "the unquiet walks of devils," who impersonate the dead in order to trouble and deceive us, and they appear mostly in graveyards because "those are the dormitories of the dead, where the devil, like an insolent champion, beholds with pride the spoils and trophies of his victory over Adam." [17] It appears then that while he has a wholesome respect for the apparition itself Browne does not believe it is a ghost, and in this respect at least he has a somewhat cooler head than most of his contemporaries.

It is interesting to note how in a superstitious age credulity breaks out at different points in different men. Sir Kenelm Digby, for example, is decidedly in advance of Browne on the subject of witches,[18] but when it comes to ghosts he stands with the absurd Alexander Ross as a champion of conservatism, and comes to the front with stories of corpses that bleed accusingly in the presence of the murderer, after the best traditions of the Elizabethan stage.[19] Both agree with More and Glanvill that spiritistic phenomena are a very important evidence for spiritual life in general. Browne does not of course deny the objective reality of apparitions. Few indeed were such hardy rationalists as to do that, and according to a well-known story Thomas Hobbes himself was not fond of going alone in the dark. But the belief that the departed soul haunts the dead body did not suit Browne's particular theology, and since the devil was for him a very real personage indeed, the given explanation satisfied the dramatic exigencies of the situation as it then existed much more completely than any remarks about a disordered mind or stomach.

The century was rife with speculations as to the relation between body and soul after death. Theoretically the church taught that there was a complete separation, but the Platonic doctrine of metempsychosis, and of the power of the body to enmesh the soul — expounded, for example, by the elder brother in Milton's *Comus* — had philosophic attractions, and the belief in ghosts was deep-rooted. Furthermore the church did not teach a final

[16] *Ibid.*, I, 37.
[17] *Ibid.*
[18] See *Observations*, Wilkin, II, 464.
[19] *Ibid.*, p. 467.

separation of the soul from the body; there was to be a resurrection of the body on the judgment day, and presumably a reunion with the risen soul. But in the meantime, according to the prevailing opinion, the soul had assumed some kind of spiritual or resurrection body at the moment of death. The status of these various bodies involved some very puzzling problems.

Browne believes that the soul is set free from the body at the moment of death, but he clings to the old idea that the body is somehow necessary to individuation, at least in the final state of the soul. He believes in the resurrection of the body on the authority of the historic church, though he confesses that it is "not inducible by reason," and admits that even if the physical body could be resurrected, it is hard to see why it should be. But he depicts with a really majestic power the dramatic moment when the "corrupted relics" of the human race, "scattered in the wilderness of forms," shall obey the powerful voice of God and stand before Him one by one in their proper shapes: "Then shall appear the fertility of Adam, and the magic of that sperm that hath dilated into so many millions." Perhaps only Donne imagines the resurrection day with like grandeur and intensity —

> At the round earth's imagined corners, blow
> Your trumpets, angels, and arise, arise
> From death, you numberless infinities
> Of souls, and to your scattered bodies go,
> All whom the flood did, and fire shall o'erthrow,
> All whom war, dearth, age, agues, tyrannies,
> Despair, law, chance, hath slain, and you whose eyes,
> Shall behold God, and never taste death's woe.[20]

The unthinkable reassembling of the myriad scattered atoms of human bodies that nature has ploughed back into her loam is for Browne one of those "wingy mysteries in divinity and airy subtleties in religion" that never stretched his *pia mater*. "I believe that our estranged and divided ashes shall unite again; that our separated dust, after so many pilgrimages and transformations into the parts of minerals, plants, animals, elements, shall at the voice of God return into their primitive shapes, and join

[20] Sonnet 7.

again to make up their primary and predestinate forms."[21] For argument he falls back on the theory that there is a persistent and indestructible individuality lodged in the material body itself which may be called its "form" — "The forms of alterable bodies in these sensible corruptions perish not; nor, as we imagine, wholly quit their mansions, but retire and contract themselves into their secret and unaccessible parts, where they may best protect themselves from the action of their antagonist."[22] And to support this strange conception he refers, as we have already seen, to a mysterious claim of the alchemists that they could restore a plant after burning it to ashes.[23]

What Browne may mean by the form of a disintegrated body it would be useless to ask. We have it on the authority of Thomas Aquinas that the soul is the form of the body. But St. Thomas seems to deny that there is any form in man but the soul.[24] Sir Kenelm Digby, a learned Catholic, takes issue with this notion of Browne's, and he advances the theory that individuality persists through dissolution in the same way that it remains unchanged by the complete bodily change of the living organism every seven years.[25] But of course this theory, too, means little or nothing to the modern mind. We are accustomed nowadays to speak of the persistence of personality, on the one hand, or of the indestructibility of matter on the other, but theories about the personality of a decayed body have no longer any intelligible meaning. Browne evidently had his doubts about this resurrection of the mysterious "form" of the body, for some years later in *Urn Burial* he proposes a different theory which is in effect like Digby's: "Severe contemplators, observing these lasting relics, may think them good monuments of persons past, little advantage to future beings. And considering that power which subdueth all things unto itself, that can resume the scattered atoms, or identify out of anything, conceive it superfluous to expect a resurrection out of relics. But the soul subsisting, other matter clothed with due accidents, may salve the individuality."[26]

[21] *Religio Medici*, I, 48.
[22] *Ibid.*
[23] Drummond had cited the same experiment (*A Cypress Grove*, p. 281).
[24] *Summa Theologica*, I, Q. 76, art. 4.
[25] *Observations*, Wilkin II, 475 ff.
[26] Chap. iii.

Besides these speculations there are certain other arguments which Browne depends on to some extent. For one thing he is always very much interested in dream psychology, which, like spiritistic phenomena, had always furnished the strongest possible proofs for animism, and Browne is thoroughly convinced that the mysterious activity of psychic powers during the suspension of the bodily is strong evidence for the existence of a soul, drugged or enmeshed in waking hours but set free in sleep. He advances his views on the matter in *Religio Medici*, in the *Letter to a Friend*, and in a special tract on dreams. This last document, a characteristically erudite little fragment, is about on a level with the views of the classical physicians in its interpretation of dreams. It concedes that the condition of the bodily organs accounts for a great many dreams, but it insists that some are undoubtedly supernatural — the visitations of devils or angels to the soul at the one time when it is free to entertain them.[27] In the *Letter to a Friend* his views seem to be more cautiously scientific. In recording the symptoms of his patient he observes that "he was now past the healthful dreams of the sun, moon, and stars, in their clarity and proper courses. 'Twas too late to dream of flying, of limpid fountains, smooth waters, white vestments, and fruitful green trees, which are the visions of healthful sleeps, and at a good distance from the grave." The fact that the sick man dreamt of his dead friends or of his own death, Browne thinks, signified nothing; it merely indicated the preoccupations of his mind. But when we turn back to *Religio Medici* we find our physician in a more mystical mood.[28] "We are somewhat more than ourselves in our sleeps, and the slumber of the body seems to be but the waking of the soul. It is the ligation of sense, but the liberty of reason; and our waking conceptions do not match the fancies of our sleeps." He believes that in the dream state he has not only freer imaginative powers, so that he can actually "compose a whole comedy, behold the action, apprehend the jests, and laugh myself awake at the conceits thereof," but that he can actually think more clearly. The only difficulty is that he cannot remember his dreams; otherwise, he says, "I would never study but in my dreams, and this time also would I choose for

---

[27] See *Works*, V, 183. (Wilkin, III, 342.)
[28] *Religio Medici*, II, 11.

my devotions." He thinks that sleepwalkers demonstrate the separation of soul from body. Hence there is a close analogy between sleep and death, for it is also true that dying men "do speak and reason above themselves; for then the soul, beginning to be freed from the ligaments of the body, begins to reason like herself, and to discourse in a strain above mortality."

These views convince him that the analogy between sleep and death is more complete than it is generally allowed to be. For both really release the psychic powers. "We term sleep a death; and yet it is waking that kills us, and destroys those spirits that are the house of life." [29] "Surely it is not a melancholy conceit to think we are all asleep in this world, and that the conceits of this life are as mere dreams to those of the next." [30]

Browne contents himself finally with one more analogy, the separate existence of the child in the womb. This seems to have been a popular contemporary argument for the soul, for we find it employed by Bacon, Donne, Davies, and Drummond, and no doubt the list could easily be added to.[31] In *Urn Burial,* where his only reference to it occurs, Sir Thomas quaintly proposes to dramatize this prenatal existence: "A dialogue between two infants in the womb concerning the state of this world, might handsomely illustrate our ignorance of the next, whereof methinks we yet discourse in Plato's den, and are but embryon philosophers." [32] There is evidence that he actually wrote such a dialogue, though no trace of it has been discovered.

This practically exhausts his specific arguments on the subject. He makes use of perhaps one other, though in a casual way, at the end of this same chapter of *Urn Burial.* Here he rests in the traditional way on the argument of the soul's aspirations, contending that "the superior ingredient and obscured part of ourselves, whereto all present felicities afford no resting contentment, will be able at least to tell us, we are more than our present selves, and evacuate such hopes in the fruition of their own accomplishments." On this argument together with his faith in the

[29] *Ibid.,* II, 12.
[30] *Ibid.,* II, 11.
[31] *Advancement of Learning,* II, ix, 3; Donne's "The First Anniversary," 453 ff.; Davies' *Nosce Teipsum,* sec. 32; *A Cypress Grove,* p. 273.
[32] Chap. iv.

Christian revelation he bases the great convictions of the fifth chapter that "there is nothing strictly immortal but immortality," and that "life is a pure flame, and we live by an invisible sun within us."

III

But the question of the soul touches Browne deeply at another point — his temperamental preoccupation with thoughts of mortality and dissolution and the awesome prospect beyond. The moment we begin to read him, almost anywhere, we enter the peculiar atmosphere of style and thought that is always associated with his name. There is one theme that is never far from his thoughts, on which he writes with the greatest intensity, and which colors all the rest — that of mortality. The theme of death invariably evokes those characteristic passages on which his fame largely rests. Much of this writing is as majestic and beautiful as anything in the English language, much of it is quaintly fantastic, but the dominant tone is somber and grave and richly melancholy. Mortality is his constant preoccupation and by far his most powerful imaginative stimulus. This is a side of Browne that so far has been ignored in these pages, but it must come to the front now as one of the fundamental traits of his character. He is more than grave or somber; there is something actually macabre in the fascination that details of death and decay and the grave exercise over him, and sometimes he even appears to be a kind of hypochondriac who is clinging against hope to Christianity.

This temperamental point of view shadows all his books. *Religio Medici* has long pages of intimate self-revelation and examinings on the subject; *Urn Burial* is deliberately keyed to a sustained expression of the mood, twining rhetorical garlands into it with elaborate art; the *Letter to a Friend* is a studied improvization, so to speak, on the same theme, and an astonishing mixture it is of tender fancy, medical theories, gruesome asides, and moral theories gratuitously intruded.

It is easy to multiply instances of this controlling preoccupation of Browne. It keeps breaking in upon almost any subject like a tolling bell. "For the world," he loves to tell us, "I count it not an inn, but an hospital; and a place not to live, but to die in." He finds "no felicity in this circle," and counts himself the "miserablest person extant" without "this reasonable moderator and equal piece of justice, death." His one scientific discovery, a substance called adipocere, is a gruesome one — it is the wax formed in coffins by decaying bodies.[33] There are very few jokes in Browne, but the most memorable are grim ones. He relishes the story that King Pyrrhus' toe could not be burnt, and besides several references to it even celebrates it in a humorous verse. This same unfortunate king inspires another whimsicality in the *Letter to a Friend*. From the subject of his consumptive patient's symptoms Browne has been irresistibly led off to talk about teeth and so into his joke: "The Egyptian mummies that I have seen have had their mouths open, and somewhat gaping, which affordeth a good opportunity to view and observe their teeth, wherein 'tis not easy to find any wanting or decayed: and therefore in Egypt, where one man practiced but one operation, or the diseases but of single parts, it must needs be a barren profession to confine unto that of drawing of teeth, and little better than to have been tooth-drawer unto King Pyrrhus, who had but two in his head." The train of thought that could lead from recording the death of a friend to King Pyrrhus' dentist by way of an aside on mummies' teeth is an eerie one even for a literary physician. In another place in the *Letter* he remarks casually that "if the bones of a good skeleton weigh little more than twenty pounds, his inwards and flesh remaining could make no bouffage, but a light bit for the grave." If one did not know Browne, or saw this only out of the context, it would seem brutal, almost like the typical *nonchalance bestiale* of the physician. But the sentence immediately following has a sudden striking dignity and elevation: "I never more lively beheld the starved characters of Dante in any living face."

Every now and then, to give another example of the strange twist in his brain, we find him lingering over gruesome Egyptian or Roman stories of the violation of dead bodies — "Surely if such depravities there be yet alive, deformity need not despair; nor will the eldest hopes be ever superannuated, since death hath spurs, and carcasses have been courted." [34] The blend of humor

[33] *Urn Burial*, chap. iii.
[34] *Vulgar Errors*, VII, xix.

and fascinated interest in the whole passage is nothing short of macabre. The first sentence he ever published, in the preface to *Religio Medici*, has already all the overtones of this music in thought and language. "Certainly that man were greedy of life, who should desire to live when all the world were at an end." The subject in hand, the unscrupulousness of the press, was prosaic enough, but mortality, his King Charles' head, could not be kept out of it.

The first intense and personal record of Browne's feelings about death is an extended passage beginning at section 38 of *Religio Medici*. He has been speaking of the resurrection and the triumph of the soul over death. Suddenly he exclaims: "This is that dismal conquest we all deplore, that makes us so often cry, O Adam, *quid fecisti*? I thank God I have not those strait ligaments, or narrow obligations to the world, as to dote on life, or be convulsed and tremble at the name of death." Then follow pages of confessions on the subject. One of the most striking is a canceled sentence found in two of the manuscripts: "It is a symptom of melancholy to be afraid of death, yet sometimes to desire it; this latter I have often discovered in myself, and think no man ever desired life, as I have sometimes death." This is a case, like Dr. Johnson's, of a man who, beneath an outward activity and normal concern with the world about him, has an inner life of lonely and somber preoccupation.

In the passage under discussion he wants to study himself. How does his pulse behave at the mention of death? It is a subject which his generation could not take calmly or lightly. Has he the detachment of a physician, or the callousness of a grave digger? He says he has not the latter at least: "Not that I am insensible of the dread and horror thereof; or, by raking into the bowels of the deceased, continual sight of anatomies, skeletons, or cadaverous relics, like vespilloes, or grave makers, I am become stupid, or have forgot the apprehension of mortality." But he feels when he holds the thing before his mind, as his generation was exhorted to do constantly, "that marshaling all the horrors, and contemplating the extremities thereof, I find not anything therein able to daunt the courage of a man, much less a well-resolved Christian." He is willing to forgive Adam, to accept nature's law, and "like the best of them, to die." And then as though to recreate this platitude, comes one of those powerful imaginative strokes of his — "to die, that is, to cease to breathe, to take a farewell of the elements, to be a kind of nothing for a moment, to be within one instant of a spirit." It is so vivid that it unrolls great reaches of thought in a second of time. We are let for that moment into the speculations of a mind that has often been imaging the instant of death, projecting itself into that empty gulf where the soul is annihilated "for a moment," for a dark blank of time. And there is the same subtlety here as when he says elsewhere that he could be "content to be nothing almost to eternity." As Dr. Johnson said, he who does not perceive the full possibilities of that "almost" little knows Sir Thomas Browne.

As he goes on we realize how much he has brooded on dissolution. "I am naturally bashful: nor hath conversation, age, or travel, been able to affront or enharden me; yet I have one part of modesty which I have seldom discovered in another, that is, (to speak truly) I am not so much afraid of death, as ashamed thereof." [35] The disfigurement, the indignity, the "disgrace and ignominy" of it appall him. It is fearful to think that friends of a moment ago are afraid of us, that animals boldly prey on us. He has thought in a storm that he would be willing to sink alone to the sea bottom, without deathbed tears of pity, or the sermons and perfunctory consolations of priests. Yet perhaps it was cynical in Diogenes to will his body to be hanged as a scarecrow, or "rodomontado" in Lucan to be content with the open sky for a tomb, and in his calmer judgment he commends, after all, "those ingenuous intentions that desire to sleep by the urns of their fathers, and strive to go the neatest way unto corruption." We feel, though, a touch of bravado in the protest that his body is a sound one, and "as wholesome a morsel for the worms as any."

He has the earnest conviction already alluded to that life is a slender thread, that "there goes a deal of providence to produce a man's life unto threescore," and that the average span is determined not so much by natural vitality as by the secret will of God. "Though the radical humor contain in it sufficient oil for seventy, yet I perceive in some it gives no light past thirty." This is a powerful figure, and the illustration that follows is a striking

[35] *Religio Medici*, I, 40.

and sinister one: "They that found themselves on the radical balsam, or vital sulphur of the parts, determine not why Abel lived not so long as Adam." In his thirtieth year he has evidently been thinking about his age, comparing it with that of Christ and of average mortality. "Let them not therefore complain of immaturity that die about thirty"; it is the fate of men and the world to be destroyed before "the period of their constitution." The thought recurs many years later in the *Letter to a Friend*. The unknown friend and patient had died at thirty; he desired no long life, Browne says, "esteeming it enough to approach the years of his Savior, who so ordered his own human state, as not to be old upon earth." Life presents itself as a gloomy mystery, a little flame fearfully easy to blow out, and he feels shadowed by dark perils like Guyon in Mammon's cave.

As a physician he knows the delicate balance of the human organism. Men stupidly "quarrel with their constitutions for being sick; but I, that have examined the parts of man, and know upon what tender filaments that fabric hangs, do wonder that we are not always so." Not only so, but "we are beholding unto every one we meet, he doth not kill us."[36] There is then only one comfort left to mortals — that anything and anyone can deprive us of life, but nothing can take away death from us.

Urn Burial carries on the same train of thought. It is a sustained and majestic meditation on the vanity of life, but also on the sobering weight and immensity of that eternity to which man must return. For one thought that always inspires Browne to really tremendous passages is the fear of annihilation. Take for example the close of the fourth chapter: "Happy are they which live not in that disadvantage of time, when men could say little for futurity, but from reason. Whereby the noblest minds fell often upon doubtful deaths, and melancholy dissolutions; with these hopes, Socrates warmed his doubtful spirits, against that cold potion, and Cato, before he durst give the fatal stroke, spent part of the night in reading the Immortality of Plato, thereby confirming his wavering hand unto the animosity of that attempt.

"It is the heaviest stone that melancholy can throw at a man, to tell him he is at the end of his nature; or that there is no

[36] *Ibid.*, I, 44.

further state to come, unto which this seems progressional, and otherwise made in vain." [37]

Or take the following remarkable commentary on Job's curse: "Adversity stretcheth our days, misery makes Alcmena's nights, and time hath no wings unto it. But the most tedious being is that which can unwish itself, content to be nothing, or never to have been, which was beyond the malcontent of Job, who cursed not the day of his life, but his nativity: content to have so far been, as to have a title to future being; although he had lived here but in an hidden state of life, and as it were an abortion." [38]

Or again this description of monism or pantheism: "A great part of antiquity contented their hopes of subsistency with a transmigration of their souls. . . . Others, rather than be lost in the uncomfortable night of nothing, were content to recede into the common being, and make one particle of the public soul of all things, which was no more than to return into their unknown and divine original again." [39] Browne manages to convey into this "uncomfortable night of nothing" and "the public soul of all things" an unforgettable bleakness. For him the whole idea was the horror of desolation.

The *Letter to a Friend* runs the gamut of emotion connected with death from gentle and tender faith to grotesque humor. And *Christian Morals* is simply a dignified and didactic reminiscence of the others. Its gnomic verses keep sounding a *memento mori* in one form or another. "Measure not thy self by thy morning shadow, but by the extent of thy grave; and reckon thy self above the earth by the line thou must be contented with under it." "Death will find some ways to untie or cut the most Gordian knots of life, and make men's miseries as mortal as themselves."

It is the inimitable play of these lights and shadows upon the thought of death that makes Browne different from any writer in the world. Taken with all his brooding on the vanity and misery of life and the attenuation of its thin-spun thread, on the fitness of early death, on the courage of martyrs and heathen reckless of death, on the horrors of decay and oblivion, Browne's books seem filled with one chief kind of music — with majestic

[37] Chap. iv.
[38] Chap. v.
[39] *Ibid.*

funeral marches to the grave. On earth there is no abiding place and no lasting memory—"But man is a noble animal, splendid in ashes, and pompous in the grave, solemnizing nativities and deaths with equal luster, nor omitting ceremonies of bravery in the infamy of his nature." [40]

IV

Browne's temperament is unusually somber and would seem so in any age. The seventeenth century has a reputation for melancholy. Whether it had more of it than the "merry" England of the Elizabethans, or than any other period, is a complicated question. It is not melancholy to realize to the full that life is short, that youth and beauty fade, that time flies and the past is beyond recall. These are the great themes, and the quality of their rendering in the arts is a test of the seriousness, intensity, and depth of an age. And here both the Elizabethans and the seventeenth century were supreme. Shakespeare, Milton, and the prose of the English Bible and Prayer Book are the greatest, and they belong to all men; but setting them aside, the literature of the whole period handled these themes with unsurpassed power and beauty, and through their entire range. This needs no long illustration. Single phrases at once come to mind that carry with them the whole genius of the writer: the close of Raleigh's *History*—"O eloquent, just, and mighty Death! whom none could advise thou hast persuaded"; or Donne's "bracelet of bright hair about the bone," or "never send to know for whom the bell tolls; it tolls for thee"; or Taylor's fading rose—"it bowed the head, and broke its stalk, and at night, having lost some of its leaves and all its beauty, it fell into the portion of weeds and outworn faces"; or Herrick's "To Daffodils"—

>Stay, stay,
>Until the hasting day
>Has run
>But to the even-song;
>And, having prayed together, we
>Will go with you along.

Or Marvell's "Coy Mistress"; and, perhaps supreme among all,

[40] *Ibid.*

Browne's wonderful *Urn Burial,* "the last great outcry of the dying Renaissance against devouring time." [41]

The Jacobean and Puritan age shared this full consciousness of mortality with the Elizabethans, as it shared their strong hold on life. The two belong together, and it is certainly true that "the meditations on the brevity of life, so numerous and so rich throughout [the seventeenth century] are not the rhetorical funguses of an age of decay . . . they tell rather of immense vitality contemplating its inevitable extinction." [42] But it is also true that the century had its own reasons for somberness in the recrudescence of religious conflict, with its bitter disorder and bloody wars and fierce passions.

As for the insistent concern with death, the modern man often forgets that our forefathers had actually a closer acquaintance with it than we. They had a far greater expectation of it, and at an earlier age; they were reminded of it oftener by charnel houses, churchyard graves, crowded sepulchral monuments, and passing bells; and they came to closer quarters with it in the ravages of plagues and the agonies of mortal disease almost unrelieved by medical aid.

Many deplored the lurid accompaniments of deathbed scenes and funerals. "Men fear death as children fear to go in the dark,"[43] Bacon said, and largely because of its embellishments. Drummond has the same feeling: "I have often thought . . . that the marble colors of obsequies, weeping, and funeral pomp (with which we ourselves limn it forth) do add much more ghastliness unto it than otherways it hath." [44] Taylor speaks in the same Stoic strain, with the calm wisdom of the Christian priest: "Take away but the pomps of death, the disguises and solemn bugbears, the tinsel, and the actings by candle-light, and proper and fantastic ceremonies, the minstrels and the noise makers, the women and the weepers, the swoonings and the shriekings, the nurses and the physicians, the dark room and the ministers, the kindred and the watchers; and then to die is easy, ready and

[41] Douglas Bush, *English Literature in the Earlier Seventeenth Century,* p. 337.
[42] *Ibid.,* p. 4.
[43] "Of Death."
[44] *A Cypress Grove.*

quitted from its troublesome circumstances." [45] Montaigne likewise had already spoken his mind to precisely the same effect: "I verily believe, these fearful looks, and astonishing countenances wherewith we encompass it, are those that more amaze and terrify us than death," and he describes the deathbed accompaniments with the same particularity.[46] He would have shared Browne's impulsive wish that he might have died "unseen, unpitied, without wondering eyes, tears of pity, lectures of morality, and none had said, *Quantum mutatus ab illo!"*

But none the less Taylor uses his full powers to keep the fact of death to the fore in all its aspects, and his manual on the art of dying, with its frontispiece of a pastor exhibiting the picture of a skeleton to a gentleman and his family, is as enthralling as his *Holy Living* is dull. One thinks too of the ostentatious piety of Walton's deathbed scenes, among them that of John Donne, that strangest figure of his day. Donne's imagination pierces the coffin itself. His lines are like a fleeting glimpse of the waving fronds and scuttling creatures in the depths of a marine pool. No one has so dramatized death. In the *Devotions* he daily analyzes with almost unbearable intensity the sensations of facing it in the ebb and flow of a dangerous illness. And there is the final bizarre gesture — the portrait of himself which he ordered and posed for, standing on an urn in his knotted shroud, and which, with more than a little bravado, he kept by him to the end so as to face the King of Terrors humbly and with Christian intrepidity.

This strong sense of the mortal plight of man and the Christian disparagement of the present life and concern for the world beyond was affected in the seventeenth century by a number of intellectual influences. Mention has already been made of certain "Asiatic" or "Gothic" strands in the prose style — tendencies toward ornateness and magniloquence, and in particular in this connection the inbred tradition of the pomp and grandeur of empire, and the obligation to "persuade the king in greatness." The themes that lent themselves to such a liturgy were death, the vicissitude of things, and the vanity of fame. From the wealth

---

[45] *Holy Dying*, VII.
[46] "That to Philosophize Is to Learn How to Die." (Florio's translation.)

of notable prose in this vein, in orations, memorial poems, funeral sermons, plays, dedications, and every kind of literature, it will be enough to quote a passage of Taylor on a royal burying ground:

"There is an acre sown with royal seed, the copy of the greatest change, from rich to naked, from ceiled roofs to arched coffins, from living like gods to die like men. There is enough to cool the flames of lust, to abate the heights of pride, to appease the itch of covetous desires, to sully and dash out the dissembling colors of a lustful, artificial, and imaginary beauty. There the warlike and the peaceful, the fortunate and the miserable, the beloved and the despised princes mingle their dust, and pay down their symbol of mortality, and tell all the world, that when we die our ashes shall be equal to kings', and our accounts easier, and our pains or our crowns shall be less." [47]

In modern prose, noble occasional pieces like the Gettysburg address are a rarity. In Browne's age the loftiness, dignity, and fitness of the courtly tradition were pervasive.

Another influence was the depth and fierceness of religious passions, inherited from the long history of bloody persecutions and martyrdoms of the preceding century, and about to culminate in civil war and the uprooting of the national life. There was the worm of the Puritan conscience and the lively fear of hellfire. Calvinism had been the prevailing theology of the English Reformation and, though now abandoned by the Church of England, had affected religious thought to the core and was still mighty. The fearful rigors of predestination, that "sweet and pleasant doctrine of damnation," had stressed the stern justice of God and the worthlessness and ill-desert of man. The spell of this doctrine, so graphically and clinically described by Burton, produced a gloomy and morbid psychology that stamps the period unforgettably in old and New England.

There was, of course, another side of the age and many Puritans as well as Anglicans felt a distaste for hellfire preaching. The Puritan fear of damnation is seen at its most dramatic in Bunyan's *Grace Abounding*. On the Anglican side we may instance William Perkins, a divine of some reputation in his day, whose preaching Fuller hands down to memory — "He would pronounce

---

[47] *Holy Dying*, Chap. I, sec. ii.

the word *Damn* with such an emphasis as left a doleful echo in his auditors' ears a good while after." [48]

In some quarters, also, *contemptus mundi* and other-worldliness were increased by the unsettling effect of the new science. It was frightening to be told that the sun does not really rise and set, that the elements are no longer four, that the changeless stars are not pure and incorruptible. Thus Drummond complains: "What have the dearest favorites of the world, created to the patterns of the fairest ideas of mortalities to glory in? . . . Is it knowledge? But we have not yet attained to a perfect understanding of the smallest flower, and why the grass should rather be green than red. The element of fire is quite put out, the air is but water rarified, the earth is found to move, and is no more the center of the universe, is turned into a magnes [magnet]; stars are not fixed, but swim in the ethereal spaces, comets are mounted above the planets . . . the sun is lost, for, it is but a light made of the conjunction of many shining bodies together. . . . Thus, sciences by the diverse motions of this globe of the brain of man, are become opinions, nay, errors, and leave the imagination in a thousand labyrinths. What is all we know compared with what we know not?" [49]

For Drummond the new science is not a conquest but a disaster. If the old landmarks are gone in this new tide, what becomes of human knowledge? In the effort to adjust the new universe to their own emotional demands, it was natural for many to fall back on the vanity of human learning and human pride and to think of scientific hypotheses as the mere flux and flood of opinion. There is a satiric edge in George Herbert's poem called "Vanity."

> The fleet astronomer can bore
> And thread the spheres with his quick-piercing mind.
> He views their stations, walks from door to door,
>   Surveys as if he had designed
> To make a purchase there. He sees their dances,
>   And knoweth long before
> Both their full-eyed aspects and secret glances.
>   . . . .

[48] *The Holy State.*
[49] *A Cypress Grove,* p. 249.

> The subtle chemic can divest
> And strip the creature naked, till he find
> The callow principles within their nest.
> There he imparts to them his mind,
> Admitted to their bedchamber, before
> They appear trim and dressed
> To ordinary suitors at the door.

Others are more conscious of man's dark ignorance here below and in moods of spiritual weariness shut their eyes on this world. Man must reject the senses (they are not the true ports of knowledge) and despise the body (it is the prison house of the soul) and wait but a little while for release and the instantaneous, beatific vision of full knowledge. The skeptical trend of science turned some of the most actively philosophical minds of the day toward mysticism. The unmystical John Donne has mystical moods of this sort. Witness the often quoted "Second Anniversary":

> When wilt thou shake off this pedantery
> Of being taught by sense and fantasy?
> Thou look'st through spectacles; small things seem great
> Below: but up into the watch-tower get
> And see all things despoiled of fallacies . . .
> In heaven thou straight know'st all concerning it,
> And what concerns it not, shall straight forget.

Many more examples could be given from Vaughan, Quarles, Traherne, and others. There is much of this in seventeenth-century prose and poetry.

Finally, there is the influence of Stoicism. We have already noted its effect upon sevententh-century thought, and this is particuarly marked in the attitude toward death. Browne comments upon the fact in *Religio Medici*. After quoting with approval Lucan's verses

> Victurosque Dei celant ut vivere durent
> felix esse mori,

he observes that "truly there are singular pieces in the philosophy of Zeno, and doctrine of the Stoics, which I perceive, delivered in a pulpit, pass for current divinity." [50] Taylor, who is saturated in the Roman philosophers, is an especially good example of this. And if we compare Montaigne's "That to Philosophize Is to Learn How to Die," Drummond's *Cypress Grove*, and Taylor's *Holy Dying*, we can easily see that all of them traverse a well-worn path. They use the same Stoic arguments and often the same illustrations.

A man can face death with equanimity, says Montaigne, if he remembers the following truths: Death is the inevitable lot. Thirty-five years is the natural span of life and he who passes it is fortunate. A surprising number of men meet sudden and accidental death, like Aeschylus who was killed by a turtle dropped on his head. The way to prepare for death is to face it boldly, to think about it, to be always booted for the journey. Graveyards and the sight of bones and skulls and funerals and mortal relics should inure and forewarn us, and are put next to churches for that purpose. Nature herself solves the problem, for she prepares us, and old age is made an easy decline. "Our religion hath no surer humane foundation than the contempt of life." Death is no more painful or fearful than being born. It is as great folly to bewail the fact that we cannot be alive a hundred years hence as that we could not live a hundred years ago. Compared with the life of stars and trees the span of human life is at best insignificant. Death is only a piece of the world's order. Life is simply a continual dying. If a man has lived one day he has seen all. It is our duty to make room for others. An ever enduring life would be intolerable, and not to have recourse to death would be the greatest of all curses. It is the terror with which men surround death that makes it terrible, and only those who die in bed surrounded by whining friends and doctors and preachers find it dreadful.

Drummond's *Cypress Grove* (1623) borrows too heavily from Montaigne, Bacon, Shakespeare, Donne and others to be very original, but it has distinct beauty and a genuine vigor of its own. Perhaps Drummond's habit of wide borrowing makes it the more typical and significant for our purpose. The main arguments are these: Death is chiefly terrible because of the trappings

---

[50] *Religio Medici*, I, 44.

and pomp with which it is surrounded. It is a part of nature. We must make room so that others may see the world's cabinet of rarities. If you complain that there will come a time when you will no longer be, why not repine because there was once a time when you were not? All the world's "ghastly wonders" must perish as well as you. Life is not good; why repine at returning to "old Grandmother dust?" "Man's life is a ball tossed in the tennis court of this world." The least thing kills him. "We should rather wonder how so fragile a matter should so long endure, than how so soon dissolve and decay." Man is never satisfied here. Sleep is a kind of death releasing the soul for a time. Greatness and knowledge are delusions, science is upsetting the world. Eternal life would be unendurable. Nature prepares the old for death by diminishing the capacity for pain. Death is terrible only because "that is ever terrible which is unknown; so do little children fear to go in the dark, and their fear is increased with tales." One year is enough to see all of life, for "days are not to be esteemed after the number of them but after the goodness," and the musician who makes the sweetest melody, not the one who plays longest, is most praiseworthy. Renown, possessions, children are wilting weeds, snow in the sun. The soul only is immortal and rises to God and eternity. Death is but "a short, nay, sweet sigh" compared to the smallest dram of the infinite felicities of heaven.

Drummond luxuriates, as Browne does, in the melancholy grandeur of this philosophy of mortality, and he makes the most of the possibilities that it affords for a Christian peroration, proceeding from the vanity of life to the glory of heaven. But the arguments for resignation and submission are Stoic. Jeremy Taylor repeats them all, with almost incomparable eloquence, as though they were an inseparable part of Christian philosophy. Man is a bubble, a morning mushroom. Every light and shadow, every height and declension preaches him a funeral sermon and calls him to see "how the old sexton time throws up the earth and digs a grave." Life is a succession of graves from the womb to the warmth of the sun, from waking to sleeping, from youth to age. We are always in death's outer chamber. We may be killed suddenly as Aeschylus was; it is the common lot. Death is a part of nature, and (here speaks the Christian theologian) a punishment for our sins. All the great lie down in the dust with the lowliest. It is proper to plant orchards to "feed our nephews with their fruit"; this is excusable, though it is but "imaginary immortality"; but man must not plan long ahead. This is not our enduring city; life is either too short, or, because sorrowful, too long. There is no felicity here, and the sadness of this life sweetens the bitter cup of death. Think always of death. Cure yourself of earthly vanities as the young monk did who visited the tomb of his beloved and wiped the moisture from the carcass with his mantle. Death is the one port from the sorrows of life, as Lucan and Seneca and many other poets have demonstrated. It is to be accepted, nay welcomed, and not to be feared, for it is no great matter. Every one can kill us, even a fly, and all men must die. We are afraid of the accompaniments of death, rather than of the thing itself. It comes easily and quickly. The span of life consists in goodness, not years. "He that would willingly be fearless of death, must learn to despise the world"; he must not love anything passionately; he must imitate the fortitude of the heathen who destroyed themselves to attain that felicity that is not to be found here. It is certain, finally, "that he that is afraid of death . . . either loves this world too much, or dares not trust God for the next."

This is almost pure Stoicism. Almost, but not quite, for it reinforces certain Christian beliefs but does not supplant others. It gives philosophical support to the attitude that life is full of misery and that death is a natural release. But Taylor and Drummond, if not Montaigne, believe profoundly also in the fall and redemption of man and in the rewards and punishments of the life beyond. Here they part company with the Stoics. Yet Stoicism, next to Christianity itself, has been the most influential of all moral philosophies throughout Western history and we almost instinctively identify ourselves with it. To take things "philosophically" means to fall back on the inner integrity, the spark of virtue in the breast, which steels the heart to accept its fate calmly, whether good or bad, and to face death and perhaps final oblivion without fear. Such a philosophy could scarcely be openly avowed in the seventeenth century but it could be, and was, a strong antidote, even for the devoutly religious, against the altogether exaggerated emphasis which the Reformers put upon human depravity and the deserved punishment of hellfire.

And the influence of Stoicism also worked in another direction. Lovers of the later Roman philosophers were affected by their pessimism, and it was easy in the seventeenth century to draw comparisons with the decadence of the Roman Empire and to fall into moods of Stoic melancholy and world-weariness. Shakespeare, to go no further, illustrates all these traits. They are very common in the literature of the period.

V

But it is time to return to Browne. To what extent was he affected by the various influences just described? As for the rhetoric of mortality, the wonderful fifth chapter of *Urn Burial* is the supreme example of it —

"Now since these dead bones have already outlasted the living ones of Methusaleh, and in a yard underground, and thin walls of clay, outworn all the strong and specious buildings above it; and quietly rested under the drums and tramplings of three conquests; what prince can promise such diuturnity unto his relics, or might not gladly say,

> Sic ego componi versus in ossa velim?

Time which antiquates antiquity, and hath an art to make dust of all things, hath yet spared these minor monuments."

Such prose, however, although it is certainly calculated "to persuade the king in greatness," is not to be discussed in terms of mere oratorical sonorities and reverberations. But Browne sometimes warms into rather conscious eloquence on this theme, as in such a passage as the following in *Religio Medici,* where rhetorical zest seems to carry him to somewhat unnatural lengths even for an excessively saturnine young man of thirty.

"At my death I mean to take a total adieu of the world, not caring for a monument, history, or epitaph, not so much as the bare memory of my name to be found anywhere but in the universal register of God. . . . As yet I have not seen one revolution of Saturn, nor hath my pulse beat thirty years, and yet, excepting one, have seen the ashes and left underground, all the kings of Europe; have been contemporary to three emperors, four grand signiors, and as many popes. Methinks I have outlived myself, and begin to be weary of the sun; I have shaken hands with delight; in my warm blood and canicular days, I perceive I do anticipate the vices of age; the world to me is but a dream or mock-show, and we all therein but pantaloons and antics, to my severer contemplations." [51]

This waving aside of monuments, the pageantry of falling empire as a setting for his own stage, and the closing *vanitas vanitatum* all seem somewhat mannered.

Browne is little affected by religious terrorism. He is not to be frightened into heaven. He is inclined to agree with Chillingworth or Whichcote that the divine requirements for salvation are few and reasonable and that heaven and hell are states of mind rather than places. "I thank God, and with joy I mention it, I was never afraid of hell, nor never grew pale at the description of that place." [52] And again, "I can hardly think there was ever any scared into heaven; they go the fairest way to heaven that would serve God without a hell; other mercenaries, that crouch unto him in fear of hell, though they term themselves the servants, are indeed but the slaves, of the Almighty." [53] This religion of fear, he observes, "indeed makes a noise and drums in popular ears," but he cannot conceal his contempt for it. As for the bugaboo of the wrath of God and man's lost estate and the unforgivable sin he dismisses them all with a rather pointed reliance on the reasonable mercy of God: "I am of a strange belief, that it is as easy to be forgiven some sins, as to commit some others. For my original sin, I hold it to be washed away in my baptism; for my actual transgressions, I compute and reckon with God but from my last repentance, sacrament, or general absolution; and therefore am not terrified with the sins or madness of my youth." [54]

Browne is not the man to cringe before God or to groan and beat his breast at the mention of election and damnation. This does not, of course, mean that he has any doubts about original

[51] *Religio Medici*, I, 41.
[52] *Ibid.*, I, 52.
[53] *Ibid.*
[54] *Ibid.*, II, 7.

sin. "It is the corruption that I fear within me," he cries, "not the contagion of commerce without me. 'Tis that unruly regiment within me, that will destroy me; 'tis I that do infect myself; the man without a navel yet lives in me. I feel that original canker corrode and devour me; and therefore *Defienda me Dios de mi,* Lord deliver me from myself, is a part of my litany, and the first voice of my retired imaginations." [55] Browne has an uncanny ability to make theology vividly real by such fantastic strokes as this. His "man without a navel" is to appear again in the quaint chapter in *Vulgar Errors* on pictures of Adam and Eve. But the question of salvation inspires neither ardor nor terror in him. His emotions in that quarter are always cool and level.

The effect of the new science upon Browne is more complex. He is intensely receptive to it, even creatively so, but he views the life of man *sub specie aeternitatis* as a tale that is almost told. The medieval part of him believes that the world is decaying and grows old. " 'Tis too late to be ambitious. The great mutations of the world are acted, or time may be too short for our designs. . . . We whose generations are ordained in this setting part of time . . . are naturally constituted unto thoughts of the next world, and cannot excusably decline the consideration of that duration, which maketh pyramids pillars of snow, and all that's past a moment." [56]

And he has his quietistic moods. "There is yet another conceit that hath sometimes made me shut my books, which tells me it is a vanity to waste our days in the blind pursuit of knowledge; it is but attending a little longer, and we shall enjoy that by instinct and infusion, which we endeavor at here by labor and inquisition." [57]

But of course Browne is not a mystic. He is always too much interested in finding out why grass is green and blood is red. A true mystic like Traherne turns from science to "felicity" as simply as a child; a philosopher like Pascal, after a bitter struggle, steers his storm-battered vessel into the port of the Catholic faith. Browne does neither. He continues to watch the germination of duckweed and to wait for the publications of the Royal Society.

[55] *Ibid.,* II, 10.
[56] *Urn Burial,* V.
[57] *Religio Medici,* II, 8.

Nor is he a skeptic. He dismisses doubts of the immortality of the soul with a rather disdainful indifference. "I remember a doctor in physic, of Italy, who could not perfectly believe the immortality of the soul, because Galen seemed to make a doubt therof. With another I was familiarly acquainted in France, a divine, and a man of singular parts, that on the same point was so plunged and graveled with three lines of Seneca, that all our antidotes, drawn from both Scripture and philosophy, could not expel the poison of his error." [58]

Many readers, feeling the cumulative weight first of his sly doubts about miracles and then of his cold and Stoic pessimism, do not hesitate to call him a masked skeptic. But surely this is to misunderstand him. He never leaves us in any doubt as to his belief in the soul and immortality. He may be baffled at finding no seat of the soul, nothing more than in the crany of a beast, but though he knows something of the mechanism, by temperament he knows more of the mystery, and this he steadfastly interprets in terms of "something in us that can be without us, and will be after us." There is to be sure the final page of *Religio Medici* with its *summum bonum* of resignation, and the strange last paragraph of *Urn Burial,* repeated in *Christian Morals,* which, allowing for all its quaint reticence, certainly seems to damn with the faintest possible praise those "pious spirits who passed their days in raptures of futurity." These passages might be taken as hints of a growing skepticism in Browne. But the context is too overwhelmingly in another spirit. All in all, he has the Christian belief in the soul, and if not an ecstatic at least a calm trust in immortality.

It must be admitted, however, that his Christian faith has its Stoical affinities. Many are chilled by his cold resignation and saturnine detachment from ordinary, warm-blooded life. Whatever his outward life may have been, there is no denying the grave austerity of his books. *Religio Medici* is a notably somber piece of philosophy even for an age of religious gloom. The typical views of death and mortality reappear in it, but in a more intense and unrelieved form. Consider such a passage as this:

"When I take a full view and circle of myself without this rea-

[58] *Ibid.,* I, 21.

sonable moderator, and equal piece of justice, death, I do conceive myself the miserablest person extant. Were there not another life that I hope for, all the vanities of this world should not entreat a moment's breath from me: could the devil work my belief to imagine I could never die, I would not outlive that very thought. I have so abject a conceit of this common way of existence, this retaining to the sun and elements, I cannot think this is to be a man, or to live according to the dignity of humanity." [59]

This reveals an evidently sincere distaste for living without any corresponding enthusiasm for the world beyond. Browne never warms to that subject, and he conveys the impression that his hope is of a very sober and philosophical variety. The deeply Stoic note of *Urn Burial* is really unrelieved by any Christian joy. "To subsist in bones, and be but pyramidally extant, is a fallacy in duration"; "the mortal right-lined circle must conclude and shut up all"; "the iniquity of oblivion blindly scattereth her poppy"— this is the incessantly reiterated cadence in chapter after chapter, with never a burst into major music, or a wave flung at last over the rocky wall. A sermon of Donne or Taylor breaks sooner or later into exultation, but *Urn Burial* never changes its harmonies. Once or twice toward the end we come upon what seems like the beginning of a triumphant peroration — "There is nothing strictly immortal but immortality," or "Life is a pure flame and we live by an invisible sun within us." But the promise is not fulfilled and each time Browne drops back into his dirge-like measures — "A small fire sufficeth for life, great flames seemed too little after death, while men vainly affected precious pyres, and to burn like Sardanapalus." Everything is keyed to the refrain of old mortality — "Mummy is become merchandise, Mizraim cures wounds, and Pharaoh is sold for balsams."

The *Letter* is pervaded by the same Stoic tone. It repeats, in a particularly harsh form, the argument of the folly of having children: "He was willing to quit the world alone and altogether, leaving no earnest behind him for corruption or aftergrave, having small content in that common satisfaction to survive or live in another, but amply satisfied that his disease should die with himself, nor revive in a posterity to puzzle physic, and make sad

[59] *Ibid.*, I, 38.

mementoes of their parent hereditary." It expatiates again on the miserable emptiness of life, and this time introduces a particularly Stoical philosophy of compromise with mundane existence: "To soften the stream of our lives, we are fain to take in the reputed contentations of this world, to unite with the crowd in their beatitudes, and to make ourselves happy by consortion, opinion, or co-existimation; for strictly to separate from received and customary felicities, and to confine unto the rigor of realities, were to contract the consolation of our beings unto too uncomfortable circumscription." It repeats the Stoical convictions formed years before that the world grows worse, that length of life is in virtue not years — " 'tis superfluous to live unto gray hairs" — carrying it so far as to maintain that conversion makes a man old. It notes with melancholy complacency that this unknown friend was willing to die at the properest age, thirty years, for Browne has often observed (and here he leaves the beaten track) that the old, far from being prepared for death, "oft stick fast unto the world, and seem to be drawn like Cacus's oxen, backward, with great struggling and reluctancy unto the grave."

The didactic and for the most part dull *Christian Morals* is like the rest. "In seventy or eighty years," says Sir Thomas, now in his calm old age, "a man may have a deep gust of the world." If he sees a little he sees all; life is "but a small parenthesis in eternity," and your man of years "having been long tossed in the ocean of this world . . . will by that time feel the indraught of another," and "wisely ground upon true Christian expectations."

In all this Browne strikingly echoes Marcus Aurelius. The *Meditations* is full of passages like these: "Of the life of man the duration is but a point, its substance streaming away, its perception dim, the fabric of the entire body prone to decay, and the soul a vortex, and fortune incalculable, and fame uncertain . . . and fame after death is only forgetfulness." [60] Or again, "Thou art a little soul bearing up a corpse, as Epictetus said." [61] Or still more strikingly, "Yesterday a little mucus, tomorrow a mummy or burnt ash." [62] "But a little while and thou shalt be burnt ashes

[60] *Meditations*, trans. C. R. Haines (Loeb Classical Library), II, 17.
[61] *Ibid.*, IV, 41.
[62] *Ibid.*, IV, 48.

or a few dry bones, and possibly a name, possibly not a name even." [63]

Of course this *contemptus mundi* is as much Christian as Stoic. The flux of things, the weary cycle of repetitions, the emptiness and insignificance of life, the unreality of the outward world — the sense of all this is as common to *Ecclesiastes* and St. Augustine as to Seneca and Marcus Aurelius. And if *Urn Burial* seems to be a reincarnation of Marcus Aurelius it is because mortality is a very old theme. There is no real Stoicism in Browne. He was repelled by its fatalism and its indifference to survival after death, and he found its ethics at once too severe and too frail. The theory that virtue is her own reward he feels obliged to characterize as "but a cold principle," too severe to exercise much sway over weak human nature. It is "nought but moral honesty." He had tried to imitate a Senecan ideal — to be virtuous without a thought of heaven or hell — and he calls the principle "a great resolution." Indeed he had discovered in himself "such inbred loyalty to virtue" that he could "serve her without a livery, yet not," he found, "in that resolved and venerable way, but that the frailty of my nature, upon an easy temptation, might be induced to forget her." And he turns to Christian faith for the support which he needs.

If Browne dwells upon death it is perhaps because he is absorbed in the thought that death is the most interesting fact about life. This is the secret of his philosophy. *Urn Burial* is not complete without *The Garden of Cyrus*. It is the mysteries of adumbration, of light enfolded in darkness, of nature's alternate kingdoms of night and day that steadily light his strange, intense fires. He believes that life is intelligible only in the light of a divine mind, and that the only basis for the divine in the world is the recognition of the spiritual in man. But he does not put these arguments into a system, or fight for them intellectually against materialism ancient or modern; rather he contemplates them serenely as inevitable and natural truths — "All things began in order, so shall they end, and so shall they begin again; according to the ordainer of order and mystical mathematics of the city of heaven."

[63] *Ibid.*, V, 33.

THAT GREAT AMPHIBIUM

VI

The great sentence just quoted is the sum of the whole matter, or at least, as its author himself might say, it is the microcosm or compendium of his mind and art. And it suggests the fittest leave-taking, since for any lover of Browne it calls to mind at once the altogether magical harmonies of the peroration to which it belongs, perhaps the loveliest closing page in any English book —

"But the quincunx of heaven runs low, and 'tis time to close the five ports of knowledge. We are unwilling to spin out our waking thoughts into the phantasms of sleep, which often continueth precogitations, making cables of cobwebs and wildernesses of handsome groves. Beside Hippocrates hath spoke so little, and the oneirocritical masters have left such frigid interpretations from plants, that there is little encouragement to dream of paradise itself. Nor will the sweetest delight of gardens afford much comfort in sleep; wherein the dulness of that sense shakes hands with delectable odors; and though in the bed of Cleopatra, can hardly with any delight raise up the ghost of a rose.

"Night, which pagan theology could make the daughter of Chaos, affords no advantage to the description of order; although no lower than that mass can we derive its genealogy. All things began in order, so shall they end, and so shall they begin again; according to the ordainer of order and mystical mathematics of the city of heaven.

"Though Somnus in Homer be sent to rouse up Agamemnon, I find no such effects in these drowsy approaches of sleep. To keep our eyes open longer were but to act our antipodes. The huntsmen are up in America, and they are already past their first sleep in Persia. But who can be drowsy at that hour which freed us from everlasting sleep? or have slumbering thoughts at that time, when sleep itself must end, and as some conjecture all shall awake again?"

This is the last variation on a theme, and the most captivating for its grace and perfection of tone and texture. But its effect upon the imagination does not depend, of course, on any mere play of fancy or prolonged virtuosity in the pursuit of the quincunx through the five senses and the five stars in the Hyades. Here once more, as in all his finest passages, Browne's symbols unfold latent meanings of the most unexpected beauty, which transcend anything in his modes of thought that seems temporary or merely strange. In every generation this night-piece casts its spell upon many a reader who has felt, with Browne, in some moment of sharp awareness, the mystery of his own being — unique and solitary in the life of the mind, but bound into nature by the cycles of sleep, the wheeling constellations, and the cosmic flow of night across the world.

In his great century Sir Thomas Browne is from one point of view the skeptic, the relentless questioner, watching both the long past and the dim future with impartial serenity, standing "like Janus in the field of knowledge," and brooding on mortality. But it becomes clearer the longer we read him that his doubts never reached so much as the portals of those larger affirmations by which he lived. In a changing world he undertook the old and magnificent quest of the changeless, with a speculative energy and poetic fire not unworthy of the greatest Renaissance men of genius at their loftiest. To interpret the spiritual world that is unfolded in his books is to follow through perilous straits and enchanted islands of thought one of the most romantic odysseys in all literary history — a solitary adventure far more eventful than anything in the actual world from which it took its departure.

Index

Account of Religion by Reason, An, 48
Advancement of Learning, The, 39, 85, 110, 154
Alchemy, 82: Browne's connections with, 20–24; use in *Religio Medici*, 113
Anatomy of Melancholy, The, 6, 74, 144
Angels, nature of, 114–17
Anglicanism, *see* Church of England
Anima mundi, 112–14
Anti-Ciceronian style, *see* Style
Antidote against Atheism, 88, 131
Aquinas, Thomas, 49, 54, 77, 95, 101, 106, 142, 152
Areopagitica, 51
Aristotle, 6, 7, 13, 80, 82–84, 96, 141–42
Arminianism, 37, 48
Ashmole, Elias, 15, 20, 21, 22, 117
Asiatic style, *see* Style
Astrology, 82, 107, 109
Attic style, *see* Style
Augustine, St., 7, 176

Bacon, Francis, 17, 38, 40, 49, 55, 61, 67, 75, 78, 84–86, 107, 110, 122, 143, 144, 154, 162

Bacon, Sir Nicholas, 126
Baroque style, *see* Style
Bartholomew (Bartholomaeus Anglicus), 11, 144
Batman upon Bartholomew, 144
Baxter, Richard, 31, 66
Bekker, Balthazar, 33
Biblical criticism: Browne and, 55, 65–66
Bloody Tenent of Persecution, The, 51
Boyle, Robert, 10, 21, 22, 125
Browne, Edward, 15, 20, 68, 143
Browne, Sir Thomas: intellectual world, 6–16; friends, 15; part in a witch trial, 25–31; disinterment and reburial of skull, 33; portraits of, 34. For further references *see* other headings.
Browne, Thomas, 69
Bruno, Giordano, 80, 115, 134
Bunyan, John, 164
Burton, Robert, 6, 144, 164
Bush, Douglas, 4, 162
Butter, Joseph, 67

Cabbala, The, 12, 57, 81, 99, 102, 103n., 120
Calvinism, 48, 54, 67, 76, 103, 164
Cambridge Platonists, 51, 76, 86–89, 120

[179]

Canby, Henry S., 129
Cary, Lucius, 2d Viscount Falkland, see Falkland
Chillingworth, William, 47, 50, 68, 171
Christian Morals: theme of mortality in, 160; Stoicism in, 175
Church of England, Browne and, 41, 53–54, 59–60, 75–76
Coleridge, Samuel T., 127
Comus, 150
Conjectura Cabbalistica, 131, 132
Copernicus, Nicolaus, 8
Croll, Morris W., 38–41
Cudworth, Ralph, 18, 67, 83, 87, 88–89, 106
Culverwel, Nathanael, 87, 99, 135
Cypress Grove, A, 23n., 154, 162, 165, 167–68

Dante, 72, 89
Davies, Sir John, 144, 146, 154
De Proprietatibus Rerum, 11, 144
De Veritate, 10
Dee, Arthur, 20
Dee, Dr. John, 12, 20
Descartes, René, 8, 76, 86, 145
Digby, Sir Kenelm, 10, 35, 47, 115, 150, 152
Discours de la Méthode, 76
Discourse of the Infallibility of the Church of Rome, 50
Donne, John, 41, 53, 151, 154, 161, 163, 166, 174
Dreams, Browne's views on, 153–54
Drummond, William, 23, 91, 152, 154, 162, 165, 167–68
Dugdale, Sir William, 15, 19

Ecclesiastical Polity, The Laws of, 48, 51
Emerson, Ralph Waldo, 138
English Literature in the Earlier Seventeenth Century, 4, 162
Epicurus, 72, 73
Eternal Peace, 112
Evelyn, John, 15, 33, 127

Fairy Queen, The, 80, 139, 144, 145
Falkland, Lucius Cary, 2d Viscount of, 47, 50
Ficino, Marsilio, 81

First Anniversary, The, 154n.
Fletcher, Phineas, 144, 145, 146
Fludd, Robert, 115, 133, 134
Fortune, Browne's attitude toward, 105–12
Fuller, Thomas, 68, 164

Galen, Claudius, 95, 96, 142, 143, 146
Galileo, 8, 89
Garden of Cyrus, The: symbolism, 55, 130, 131–32, 177; botanical interest, 128–29; concept of plastic nature, 132–38; religious meaning, 176, 177–78
Gilbert, William, 8, 9, 122
Glanvill, Joseph, 21
Gosse, Sir Edmund, 15n., 16n., 20n., 27, 35, 53, 127
Gothic style, *see* Style
Grace Abounding, 164

Hale, Sir Mathew, 25–31
Hales, John, 50, 70
Harvey, William, 8, 9, 89, 98, 124, 125, 128, 143
Hazlitt, William, 35, 53
Helmont, Jean Baptiste van, 22, 143
Helvetius, Dr. John Frederick, 20
Herbert, George, 165
Herbert of Cherbury, Edward Herbert, Lord, 10
Heresies, Browne and, 62–64
Hermes Trismegistus, 22, 23, 43, 54–55, 57, 82, 120, 130
Herrick, Robert, 161
Historical Essay, 26
History of the Royal Society, 11, 21, 24
Hobbes, Thomas, 12, 66, 76, 86, 89, 101, 106, 150
Holy Dying, 161, 162, 164, 167, 168–69
Holy State, The, 164–65
Hooke, Robert, 128
Hooker, Richard, 18, 48–49, 54, 75, 76, 77
Humanism, 77
Hume, David, 66
Hutchinson, Francis, 26
Huxley, Thomas, 12, 19
Hydriotaphia, see Urn Burial
Hylozoism, 80, 98

Il Penseroso, 82

INDEX

James, William, 56
Johnson, Samuel, 157, 158
Jowett, Benjamin, 133
Justin Martyr, 133

Kant, Immanuel, 67, 111, 112
Kepler, Johannes, 89

Lamb, Charles, 59, 131
Laud, William, 48
Laws, of Plato, 105
Le Chevalier Thomas Browne, 52n., 62n., 125n.
Leroy, Olivier, 52n., 62n., 125n.
L'Estrange, Sir Hamon, 15
Letter to a Friend, A: on dreams, 153; theme of mortality in, 155, 156, 159; Stoicism in, 174
Letts, Malcolm, 25
Leviathan, 76, 89
Liberty of Prophesying, The, 51
Lipsius, Justus, 38
Lucretius, 68, 80
Luther, Martin, 77

Macrocosm, 79, 112, 140
Marcus Aurelius, 101, 175, 176
Marvell, Andrew, 161
Meditations, The, of Marcus Aurelius, 101, 175
Meyrick, Canon F. J., 34n.
Microcosm, Browne's conception of, 117–20, 140, 147
Milton, John, 51, 62, 64, 76, 77, 79, 81, 82, 102, 144, 150
Milton: Man and Thinker, 62n., 103n.
Montaigne, Michel de, 12, 38, 39, 163, 167
More, Henry, 31, 87–88, 131, 132, 135
More, Sir Thomas, 91
Mortality, theme of: in Browne, 155–61; in seventeenth century, 161–63; literary style and, 163; Puritanism and, 164; science and, 165–66; Stoicism and, 166–70; effect of these influences on Browne, 170–76
Muret, Marc Antoine, 38
Mysticism, Browne and, 43, 54, 56, 120, 138, 139, 172

Nature, Browne's conception of: in *Religio Medici*, 89–120; in *Vulgar Errors*, 120–26; in *The Garden of Cyrus*, 126–39
Neo-Platonism, 12, 81, 102
New Atlantis, The, 122
Newman, John Henry, Cardinal, 138
Newton, Sir Isaac, 10, 66, 89
Nosce Teipsum, 144, 146, 154
Notestein, Wallace, 26, 33
Novum Organum, 39, 144

Observations, 35, 150n., 152n.
Oldenburg, Henry, 15

Paracelsus, Philippus, 12, 23, 119, 148
Paradise Lost, 80, 81, 102, 144
Pascal, Blaise, 53, 172
Paston, Sir Robert, 20
Pater, Walter, 35
Perkins, William, 164
Persecution, Browne on, 68
Philo, 81, 115, 132, 134
Physiology in the Renaissance, 142–43
Pico della Mirandola, 81
Plato, 105, 133, 141–42
Platonism, 79, 120
Platonists, *see* Cambridge Platonists
Plotinus, 81
Power, Henry, 15, 128–29, 143
Pseudodoxia Epidemica, see *Vulgar Errors*
Psychology: classical and Christian doctrines of the soul, 141–42; theory in the Renaissance, 143–46; Browne's theories, 148–49
Puritanism: development and general character, 45–51; Browne and, 63–64, 69–70, 75, 171–72; its religious terrorism, 164–65
Purple Island, The, 144, 145, 146
Pythagoreanism, 43, 127, 130

Quarles, Francis, 166
Quincunx, 127, 130

Rabelais, François, 39
Raleigh, Sir Walter, 161
Rational Theology in the Seventeenth Century, 35n.
Religio Medici: style, 41, 170; mysticism in, 43, 54, 56, 120, 172; liberal spirit, 45; general character, 51; on faith and reason, 51–57; charity and

[181]

tolerance, 57–62; Browne's heresies, 62–65; biblical criticism, 65–66; on atheism, 67; on persecution, 68; on martyrdom, 68; on salvation of heathen, 70–73; contempt for the crowd in, 73–75; concept of nature, 89–105; on Fortune, 105–12; *anima mundi*, 112–14; nature of angels, 114–17; the microcosm, 117–19, 147; the soul and life after death, 148–52; on dreams, 153–54; analogy of the child in the womb, 154; theme of mortality in, 155–59; rhetoric of mortality, 170–71; attitude toward religious terrorism, 171–72; toward the new science, 172–73; toward Stoicism, 173–74
Religion of Protestants, The, 50
Resurrection of the body, Browne's views on, 149–52
Rosicrucianism, 82, 132
Ross, Alexander, 150
Royal Society, The, 8, 11, 15, 20, 24

St. Peter Mancroft, Church of, 33
Salvation of heathen, Browne's view of, 70–73
Sandys, George, 47
Saurat, Denis, 62n., 103n.
Scholasticism, 10, 11, 55, 79, 82–84, 94
Second Anniversary, The, 166
Selden, John, 12, 47
Seneca, 38–39, 176
Shakespeare, William, 77, 104, 161
Sir Thomas Browne (Gosse), 15n., 16n., 20n., 53n.
Skepticism in Browne, 44, 66, 173
Soul, *see* Psychology
Spenser, Edmund, 79–81, 144–45
Sprat, Thomas, 11, 20, 24, 97
Stephen, Leslie, 35
Stoicism: influence on prose style, 38; Browne and, 67, 73, 74, 109, 173–76; vogue in seventeenth century, 166–70
Strachey, Lytton, 35, 129n.
Style: Browne's, 37–41, 170; anti-Ciceronian, 38; Asiatic, 38, 163; Attic, 38–39; Bacon's, 38–40; Gothic, 39, 163; baroque, 40
Suckling, John, 47, 48
Summa Theologica, 101n., 107n., 142n., 152n.

Swedenborg, Emanuel, 138
Symbols, Browne's use of, 54, 138

Table Talk, 47
Taine, Hippolyte Adolphe, 6, 37
Taylor, Jeremy, 51, 68, 161, 162, 164, 167, 168–69, 174
Tertullian, 42, 54
That to Philosophize Is to Learn How to Die, 163, 167
Theatrum Chemicum, 20, 21
Tildesley, M. L., 34n.
Timaeus, 133
Tolerance in Browne, 64, 68–70
Tract Concerning Schism and Schismatics, 50
Traherne, Thomas, 166, 172
Transactions of the Royal Society, 8
Trismegistus, *see* Hermes Trismegistus
True Intellectual System of the Universe, The, 88
Tulloch, John, 35
Tyler, Dorothy, 26
Tyndall, John, 79

Underhill, Evelyn, 138
Urn Burial: symbolism, 4, 55; on salvation of heathen, 72–73; theme of mortality in, 155, 159, 160; style, 170; Stoicism in, 174
Ussher, James, 64
Utopia, 91

"Vanity," 165
Vaughan, Henry, 166
Vesalius, Andreas, 143, 149
Vincent of Beauvais, 11
Vulgar Errors: as a scientific work, 6–9, 16–19; view of proletariat, 74; concept of nature, 121–26; theme of mortality in, 156

Walton, Izaak, 163
Wellek, René, 40
Westcott, Brooke Foss, 57
Whichcote, Benjamin, 61, 87, 171
White, Andrew D., 101
Williams, Roger, 51
Winter's Tale, The, 104
Witchcraft, Browne's views on, 31–33

Zohar, The, 99n., 103n.

www.ingramcontent.com/pod-product-compliance
Lightning Source LLC
Chambersburg PA
CBHW061447300426
44114CB00014B/1879